GW00320020

STATE SECRETS

Behind the scenes of the 20th century

Chris Pomery

the national archives

Acknowledgements

My thanks go to my editor, Sheila Knight, who came up with the concept of this book and who did a huge amount of work to identify suitable stories and track down documents. In doing so she helped make this book not just a challenge but a pleasure to write. Needless to say, any oversights, omissions and mistakes are my own.

First published in 2006 by
The National Archives, Kew, Richmond, Surrey, TW9 4DU, UK
www.nationalarchives.gov.uk

The National Archives was formed when the Public Record Office and Historical Manuscripts Commission combined in April 2003.

A catalogue card for this book is available from the British Library.

ISBN 1 905615 04 3
978 1 905615 04 9

Jacket designed by Briony Chappell

Printed in the UK by CPI Bath Press

Picture sources Images can be seen at the National Archives unless stated otherwise.
p. 1 INF 3/237; p. 5 INF 3/1050; p. 10 and 29 INF 3/1026; p. 17 Topham Picturepoint, Topfoto.co.uk; p. 23, 41, 54, 103, 120 Punch Ltd, www.punch.co.uk;
p. 43 INF 3/1176; p. 46 INF 2/73; p. 61 www.CartoonStock.com; p. 72 KV 4/284;
p. 83 INF 3/1150; p. 96 INF 3/958; p. 101 INF 3/913; p. 113 Mary Evans Picture Library;
p. 128 INF 3/1104; jacket front INF 3/1325; jacket back INF 13/217

CONTENTS

THE COMMON THREAD running through this book is that nearly all of the documents cited have been opened for the first time to public view at the National Archives in the past few years.

Archived documents come in all shapes and sizes, and they can take time to decipher. But they can reach out over the intervening gap of time to touch you as well. This shock hit me when I realized that the terse margin notes initialled 'W.S.C.' meant that the wartime cabinet papers in my hand had been read first by Winston Churchill himself.

Another surprise is that some of these stories aren't just history but are still alive. In August 2006 the Secretary for Defence, Des Browne, announced that he was seeking a blanket pardon for the 306 troops who were executed by the British during World War One (see p. 88). And only the previous month the Metropolitan Police asked to review their old files about the original seller of prime ministerial honours, Arthur Maundy Gregory, to help them in their most recent investigations (see p. 91).

There are more than one hundred million documents held in the National Archives. Any visitor with proof of identity can get a free reader's ticket to access them. The catalogue codes at the foot of each story indicate the files that I've used. You can find out how to access them by reading 'Finding out more' on p. 128.

Chris Pomery

RED-FACED OFFICIALS

The headache of state occasions

The four funerals of monarchs in the last century, and the five coronations, all encountered problems, which were faithfully catalogued by officials from the Ministry of Works and its predecessor office.

On the death of Edward VII in 1910 the main issue was the number of wreaths that could be placed upon the coffin, which was restricted to four, including one from the royal family, plus one each from the Commons and the Lords. That left the fourth spot vacant and a potential diplomatic minefield. In the end, the vacancy was offered to the late king's cousin, Kaiser Wilhelm II of Germany, a gesture that seems ironic given the state of international relations in the rest of that decade.

The coronation of George V and Queen Mary in 1911 faced a major seating shortage. This was solved by the erection of an annexe at the west end of Westminster Abbey and galleries of temporary seating. Officials were so concerned about the soundness of the structure that 200 men from the Brigade of Guards were detailed to test it.

The funeral of George V in 1936 was complicated by the enforced cross-country journey from Sandringham in Norfolk, where the king had died, to Windsor in Berkshire, where his funeral took place. When the funeral cortege set out from King's Cross Station to

Westminster Hall for the lying-in-state, the rattling of the horse-drawn carriage dislodged an orb on the imperial crown, which had to be retrieved from the roadside.

Officials roundly complained that MPs took advantage of their privilege to invite four guests each to view the king's body without the need to queue in an attempt to turn the lying-in-state into a vote-winning exercise. 'Certain members … introduced large numbers of constituents resulting in congestion in the crypt,' the report huffily notes. The proclamation of George V's son, Edward VIII, in 1936, was drowned out by a 41-gun salute in nearby St James's Park, a venue chosen over the more distant Hyde Park.

The lying-in-state in 1952 of George VI, the younger brother of Edward VIII who took the throne after the latter's abdication in 1936, was plagued by a leaky roof through which rain dripped on to the platform supporting the catafalque. Having got away with it some sixteen years before, MPs once again abused their privileges by inflating the number of guests they brought in.

Many files detail the half year of preparations for the present Queen's coronation in 1953. The Colonial Office was locked in protracted discussions with the Earl Marshal about the order of precedence among the '300 representatives of the Colonial Empire' who were invited to Westminster Abbey. There is a note that the contents of the inch-thick file should be cross-referenced 'under Native Rulers'. Of particular interest was how the order among multiple Malayan sultans should be arrived at, which was eventually decided according to the number of guns used in the salute that the Royal Navy granted each one.

This coronation was the first major ceremonial of the television age, albeit in black and white on tiny screens. The country was still gripped by post-war austerity, and it appears that Westminster Abbey was caught short in one respect. The official report noted drily that 'it was found, early on Coronation Day, that much of the lavatory paper had been removed, and in future it will be necessary to take special steps to prevent this'.

The Colonial Office's job was not done yet. A report in the *Sydney Morning Herald* in Australia had mistakenly listed one of the Abbey attendees as 'the Princess of the Pitcairn Islands'. This was news to the remote Pacific islanders, descendants of the mutineers of the *Bounty*, who knew they had none such. In July 1953 the islands' magistrate, John Christian, wrote to the Governor's secretary in Suva, Fiji, to complain. The wheels turn slower in the tropics and it was not until September that Suva contacted London, commenting that Christian was right and that the lady's family had been resident on Tahiti for 100 years. 'The Pitcairners are indignant that she should have been allotted a seat in the Abbey when the Chief Magistrate was only offered a seat in one of the stands on the route,' the governor noted, before adding wearily: 'You will, I feel sure, appreciate that this is another of Pitcairn Island's tremendous trifles.'

LEWDNESS IN HYDE PARK

It was an annual summer problem for the keepers of London's parks: how to prevent lewd behaviour.

In the 1930s the focus was the bathing area in the Serpentine in Hyde Park. Men swimming for free in the public area were slipping into the paid area where female bathers were allowed. With only two policemen on duty, the situation became unmanageable on hot days. On 10 July 1932 mixed bathing was allowed during some very hot weather and 4,000 people turned up. The subsequent police report complained that people 'swarmed all over the water … some swam under the bridge into Kensington gardens [undressing] in full view of hundreds of persons. The people paid not the slightest attention to any of the regulations.' It took eight policemen to restore order.

The police concluded that 'there should be no means of access between the free bathing and the mixed bathing areas. It is in the former area that most of the rowdy element congregate who, after undressing, have free access to the mixed bathing area.' They also urged that it was necessary to erect a railing to keep 'undesirable persons of both sexes' away from the women's changing tents. Some rules were relaxed though: 'no objection is raised to male bathers on shore lowering the costume to the waist' for the purpose of sunbathing, one report notes.

The police were reluctant to reduce their numbers, but HM Office of Works, which was responsible for the parks, was anxious to cut costs, complaining in the following September that 'the average weekly expenditure has, in fact, been well in excess of the receipts'.

The 1930s were characterized by large-scale changes in bathing rules, each one causing ever more distress to the harassed park policemen forced into pointless endeavours that were doomed to failure. In 1932, for example, the free bathing area was reduced by half to make more space available for boating. This resulted in a flood of swimmers moving outside the restricting buoys and meant that rowers were able to run up alongside bathers. 'Pandemonium' was the police verdict.

In 1936 Sunday bathing was still banned between 10 am and 2 pm, the hours of churchgoing. Children were not allowed to bathe, so they spent their time trying to do so, which meant that the police were 'fully occupied in endeavouring to prevent children from entering the water'. In exasperation, the police suggested extending the hours of bathing, and a week later the Office of Works resignedly complied.

Another problem was that young girls were kept apart from boys, but only by being herded into the area with paying adults, which was unfortunately 'frequented by undesirables of a certain type, from whose company young girls should, if possible, be kept'. The regulations also separated parents from their children, which encouraged bathing outside of the designated area as parents opted to keep an eye on their offspring without getting into the water.

The Second World War only loosened attitudes, but by the 1960s it was apparent that standards were in danger of serious slippage. A parliamentary secretary recorded in 1964 that 'it can only be a matter of time before the first topless bathing suit makes its appearance at the Serpentine Lido' and expressed the hope that the attendants would know how to combat such an eventuality. Apparently they didn't, as the bailiff of the royal parks issued an instruction a week later.

Immorality was rife on the grass. One out-of-town schoolmaster visitor to the capital in 1963 wrote angrily that park attendants 'are just open air brothel keepers', and the following year the Inspector of Parks reminisced that 'when I first started as a park keeper in Greenwich park in 1945 there was an order (unofficial I'm afraid) that all persons laying on the grass would lie apart and we did enforce the order. I dread now to think what would have happened if we had been challenged in a court as to our authority for doing this.'

Wartime search for female friskers

Women travellers were routinely waved through customs at Britain's ports and airports in the early decades of the last century because officials feared a ruckus if they were searched. Customs documents reveal that this laissez-faire policy was linked to a traumatic pre-war experience suffered by an overzealous official who once had the temerity to ask the Countess of Winchelsea to open her topcoat.

Official frustration at the ease with which half the population could smuggle materials through Britain's borders led to some impromptu solutions. In the busy port of Liverpool, suspicious customs officials routinely asked an elderly woman from the landing-stage tearoom to frisk female passengers for contraband. Astonishingly, the files suggest that several major ports had no female staff available to search women passengers until 1942 despite, as one official pointed out, the increase in their workload now that they had to clear everyone leaving the country as well as entering it.

The lamentable state of affairs in Liverpool was set out in a plaintive confidential memorandum of December

1940, sent to customs headquarters in London by B.J. Herrington, the port's waterguard superintendent. Noting that the landing-stage refreshment room had been closed, Superintendent Herrington wrote that the 'only females handy are members of the Censors' staff who are hardly the type of person we require' and that he now had to wait for a policewoman to travel from the local prison. Clearly the police resented this requirement. A local superintendent observed that, in his opinion, their line of work had accustomed them to 'handling low women' and as a consequence they 'became coarsened'. He suggested Herrington contact 'widows of higher police officials', who might be the right type.

Superintendent Herrington was certainly looking for a person of a somewhat superior type: 'At the actual search the female searcher would necessarily be working without official supervision, and having regard to the fact that women of refinement and high social standing may occasionally be under treatment, I feel that we should have a searcher who would be decent as well as persistent.'

His superiors in London were unimpressed and, despite the threat posed by Hitler, seemed more concerned with appearances than effectiveness. The inspector-general of the waterguard, C.M. Woodford, replied that usually 'the power to invoke readily the services of a woman searcher was at most a possibly dangerous tool to leave in the hands of the zealous seizure maker. It is well known that women rely on the rarity of the search to smuggle on the person but it was better to risk the loss of a comparatively modest amount of duty than a first class row which might easily result from suspicion (well grounded) leading to the search of an innocent woman.' Clearly a man scarred by experience, he added: 'I have a keen recollection of the quarrel we had with the Earl of Winchelsea ...'

Officials on the ground battled on as best they could. In December 1940 the Liverpool customs picked up two French women who had tried to smuggle £1,600 in gold coins and bonds on board a ship bound for America. They had stitched them into their clothing. One official cited, 'as an example of what a woman will do', the story of one 'who recently concealed three £500 notes in the possibly most inaccessible and unsuspected part of her body. Only a woman and a well coached woman could have found the booty.' He concluded that 'What is wanted for this delicate and important work is not the sort of superior caretaker odd jobber', and suggested that £4 a week should secure the services of the right kind of woman.

Only after the situation was reviewed by the Swinton Committee within the War Cabinet was change pushed through, though. The first full-time female frisker did not arrive in Liverpool until April 1942.

CUST 106/432/1–2

14

Wilson's miniskirt research

Labour Prime Minister Harold Wilson, once one of Oxford's youngest economics dons, famously called for the transformation of Britain in the 'white heat of revolution', by which he meant through science and technology rather than Marxism. He is remembered for founding the Open University, and promoting higher level research and development. Yet ironically, his administration attracted more attention for what has gone down in history as 'the miniskirt project'.

The funding regime for research at higher institutions had been changed by the arrival in 1965 of the Social Science Research Council (SSRC). Armed with a remit to assist research into economics and an initial budget in 1966/7 of £590,000, officials had high hopes of raising this figure to £4.6 million by 1972/3.

These plans came slightly unstuck in 1968, when the national press latched on to a very small one-year project costing £1,432 that had been approved by the SSRC's Psychology Committee. This body had decided to fund a Dr Gibbons at Newcastle University to study how fashions arise. In the words of the project proposal, it was 'a study of the communications aspect of clothes and the effect of attitudes towards them of the similarity of the communication conveyed to them and the impression of the self which it is deemed to communicate'. In the shorthand of the press, however, government money was being spent on working out why men prefer girls in short skirts.

Wilson appears to have been alerted to this particular project by the reports in the press and his initial enquiry elicited a justification from the SSRC, carefully ticking all the boxes, which explained that 'economically, clothing manufacture and fashion change involve immense industries, and changes in fashion can spell prosperity or disaster for large numbers of small businesses, and can have an important effect on exports'. Perhaps a little overconfidently, it went on to claim that 'Dr Gibbons hopes that his research will be the first step towards the development of a predictive theory of fashion change'.

The accomplished statistician in Harold Wilson was piqued. The SSRC's response elicited a flurry of comments in his neat green biro, all of which were added to a growing file of correspondence between his office and the Department of Education and Science (DES). 'If this is <u>so</u> valuable to these vast industries why do they not pay for it,' he noted, before adding with a touch of innocence that in the current age of spin seems lost to us forever: 'Another point. How did this get to the Press. His PR suggests he's a very odd & extrovert character.'

DES officials were up to the challenge of the first question, countering that 'it will be necessary to show evidence … before the interest of the business world can be aroused'. In answer to the second, perhaps touchier, query, they pointed the finger at the university, which had briefed the local press. One K.A. Strutt, assistant personal secretary to the minister, Michael Stewart, commented that 'Dr G is reported to be appalled by the outcome of his interview with the press, and strenuously denies that he made any mention of mini-skirts as the object of his research'. In a silent rebuke, the file contains an article from the *Guardian* that contradicts this last claim.

Clearly, Dr Gibbons' research did not lead to a universal theory of fashion adoption or otherwise we would have heard about it, but Wilson's glance, once focused, was not so easily diverted. Notes in the margins indicate that he asked for the growth rate of SSRC spending to be cut back.

The man who famously coined the phrase 'a week is a long time in politics' would not be surprised to learn that the present-day Economic and Social Research Council presides over an annual budget in excess of £100 million to support tertiary level research and postgraduate training, has a remit to focus on empirical issues, and publishes special 'plain English' versions of its programmes.

....

The 'Yes, Minister!' diaries

The Crossman diaries were a revelation when published
in 1975. The three volumes on Richard Crossman's ministerial career 1964-70 laid bare for the first time
the inner workings of government. Dying of cancer in
1974, Crossman had appointed another left- wing Labour
minister, Michael Foot, as his literary executor.

Foot quickly ran into opposition. 'There will
inevitably be problems since the diary contains a
blow by blow account of many cabinet discussions,'
noted the Cabinet Secretary, Sir John Hunt. The head
of the civil service, Sir William Armstrong,
concurred. 'Mr Crossman breaks a tradition of mutual
trust and, for that matter, of good manners. In my
view, nothing would be the same again.'

Hunt, preparing for a business trip to the USA,
informed Prime Minister Harold Wilson that if negoti-
ations with Crossman's literary executors failed, the
Treasury Solicitor would seek a last-minute injunction
to prevent publication. This was thwarted when the
Sunday Times brought forward the serialization of the
book. Hunt's memo was probably on Wilson's desk when
the weekend papers arrived, for the PM's neat hand has
written across the top 'we have been overtaken'.

The BBC series *Yes, Minister!* was supposedly inspired
by the quotation: 'The Civil Service is profoundly
deferential - "Yes, Minister! No, Minister! If you
wish it, Minister!"'

18

GOVERNMENT PLAN TO AXE CENOTAPH SERVICE

In the mid-1970s Home Office officials flirted with the idea of axing the annual Remembrance Day service at the Cenotaph in London.

The question arose when the Home Office was in the process of moving from its offices opposite the Cenotaph in Whitehall to St Anne's Mansions. The bottom three floors were required on Remembrance Day to host the largest concentration of dignitaries regularly seen in the capital. With the building out of commission, might not this be an opportune time to cancel not only the next ceremony but the whole commemoration for good?

The first doubt had been raised by the church in 1966. It felt that the Cenotaph service had become too backward looking and had little real meaning for the younger generation. It wanted a more inclusive ceremony that would remember not just the dead of the two world wars but everyone who had died in the name of humanity, a change instinctively resisted by officials who feared it would lengthen the service. The idea was ruled out by the Labour Home Secretary, Jim Callaghan, who said the country was not ready for such a change.

Faced with their impending logistical problem in 1973, officials looked first at a permanent move for the imposing monument of Portland stone designed by Sir Edwin Lutyens and erected in 1920. The Home Office could find no record of why the Cenotaph was situated outside their offices, as the ministry had not assumed responsibility for the annual ceremony until 1924. Building experts, meanwhile, said it could not be moved without risking permanent damage. Officials for their part ruled out both handing responsibility over to the building's proposed new tenants, the Foreign Office, and the temporary relocation of the ceremony.

Files report that the Queen wished the service to continue unchanged, though she 'accepted that the time might come when it no longer commanded adequate public interest, and was inclined to think that when that time arrived it might be well to consider abandoning it altogether'.

The British Legion wanted to change the wording so that it referred to all dead from all conflicts, not just the two world wars. They were also concerned that the two-minute silence was no longer observed across the country as it had once universally been. Officials knew that the only person who could utter an 'inspirational appeal' to keep the silence was the Queen. However, they were 'reluctant to suggest it to her unless we could be assured of its effect'. Such a fear of failure did not extend to the Archbishop of Canterbury, to whom they passed that particular buck.

Sir Arthur Peterson, permanent under-secretary of state at the Home Office, thought the service would not survive a change of venue to Westminster Abbey. 'A ceremony of this kind should be based upon some spontaneous feeling, or it is worthless,' he opined, blithely ignoring one of the key recommendations for it, that of tradition.

Pressure for change was also coming from various other quarters. It was noted that removing some of the Commonwealth aspects might give the ceremony a 'more European slant, and what with present controversies' – Britain was negotiating to join the EEC in 1975 – 'this would not appear altogether an appropriate time for such a transition'.

The Scottish National Party leader, Douglas Henderson, put the cat among the pigeons by asking to attend. Officials feared that he would want to lay a wreath and were concerned not only that all the other small parties might want to do the same but also that the SNP might hijack the service by laying a wreath for Scotland. A working party, by now busy considering the future of the ceremony, came down in favour of a single collective wreath. Framing a reply to the SNP, the Home Office stated that the request could be turned down as 'representation at the Cenotaph is properly confined to leaders of parties operating throughout the UK'.

Thirty years on and the annual service at the Cenotaph, held on the second Sunday in November – the closest to the exact moment the First World War Armistice came into effect at the eleventh hour of the eleventh day of the eleventh month of 1918 – is enjoying something of a resurgence. The working party eventually decided to make the ceremony more inclusive by honouring civilian services such as fire and police.

In recent years the service hit the headlines in 1982, when Labour leader Michael Foot wore over his suit a garment the popular press unkindly described as a 'donkey jacket'. Foot defended himself by citing the Queen Mother, who had described it as a good choice of clothing against the November cold. But the image of the stooping Foot probably sealed his unelectability in the mind of the electorate.

Poppy Day remains a visible tradition across the country, and the growth of popular interest in history, combined with major anniversaries connected with the Second World War, has refuelled interest in the November observance.

HO 342/86

Curing Saddam's bad back

In 1975 Britain, like other Western governments, was courting Iraq's ruling Ba'ath Party and was eager to sell it Lynx helicopters. So when Ambassador John Graham heard from his Finnish counterpart that strongman Saddam Hussein had severe back problems, he got a quick response from Terry Clark of the Foreign and Commonwealth Office's Middle East Department.

'If Sadaam is suffering from a broken disc pinching the sciatic nerve there is an operation, by name a laminectomy, regularly and successfully undertaken in various hospitals in the UK, by which there is a very good chance of total recovery.'

It's not clear if our man in Baghdad ever got the chance to offer the services of the NHS to the future Iraqi president, though Saddam continues to complain of back pain during his trial in Baghdad.

CUNNING PLANS AND HARE-BRAINED SCHEMES

Hollowood

Princess Elizabeth to woo the Welsh

One of the strangest ideas dreamt up to secure the home front in the months before the outbreak of the Second World War was a proposal in 1939 to make the 12-year-old Princess Elizabeth the head of a newly created Duchy of Cymru, a title loosely associated with Wales' distant past.

The idea was floated in a letter to the Home Secretary, Herbert Morrison, by a self-appointed constitutional expert, Edward Iwi, as a way of taking the wind out of the sails of the growing Welsh nationalist movement. Citing as evidence an arson attack on an RAF depot in Caernarvonshire in 1936, Iwi warned the government that nationalists active in north Wales might form an alliance with Irish republicans and become a potential threat in wartime.

Morrison's officials rejected the Duchy plan for fear of arousing the 'perennial jealousy between North and South Wales'. Iwi's other suggestion, that the Princess become the Constable of Caernarvon Castle (a largely ceremonial post then held by former prime minister Lloyd George), was also rejected on the grounds that the castle was a symbol of English repression.

A third idea, that the Princess could tour the country as patron of the Urdd Gobaith Cymru, the Welsh League of Youth, turned out to be even less appropriate. The Urdd had been set up in 1922 to promote the Welsh language and, like many youth movements across Europe at the time, ran a fine programme of mass-participation gymnastics. Its founder, Sir Ifan ab Owen Edwards, approved the idea, but it was quickly dropped when King George V pointed out that some of the Urdd's leaders were pacifists and that therefore the Princess could not possibly share a platform with them. A sceptical Morrison noted in the margins of the proposal: 'I feel some reluctance to suggest a scheme which involves harnessing the poor child at so early an age to the chariot of royal duties.'

Iwi seems to have been regarded as a gadfly by the British government; on several occasions he highlighted royal protocol issues that the government had overlooked, including one in 1946 that almost saw the inadvertent creation of a British regency. He created a flurry of irritation in 1959 by suggesting in a letter that the soon-to-be-born Prince Andrew would be severely disadvantaged as, following a 1952 proclamation on the royal title, he would bear his mother's maiden name of Windsor rather than her husband's name of Mountbatten. Iwi's suggestion that the little prince would thus be lumbered with 'the badge of bastardy' roused a senior member of the Lord Chancellor's office to comment that 'Mr Iwi has fallen below his usual standards: his thesis is not only hopelessly misconceived but also in the worst of taste ... he must be silenced'. Senior advisors and Number 10 plotted the safest line of defence: that members of the royal family have no surname and their position is 'in no way analogous to that of subjects'. A discreet letter from the Prime Minister's office asked Iwi to lay off the topic and a proclamation clarified the situation the following year.

'The trouble with Iwi is that he usually puts his finger on an awkward question,' noted the Lord Chancellor's private secretary, Sir George Coldstream, who later commented that 'one is sorely tempted to cane him for being so cheeky'.

HO 144/22915 LCO 2/8112

· ·

Poisoned walnut whips

In November 1922 the Commissioner of the Metropolitan Police, Brigadier-General Sir William Horwood, received some chocolates in the post. Thinking they were from his daughter Beryl, he tucked into them after lunch. The Commissioner was later found writhing on the floor in pain, though he still had the presence of mind to retain the packaging.

The culprit was identified as one Walter Tatam. The file does not explain his motive, but he clearly held a deeply felt grudge against the police. Not only had he sent walnut whips laced with weedkiller to Commissioner Horwood, but he had also posted poisoned chocolate éclairs to other senior members of the Met.

Pigeon strike force mothballed

In the event of a third world war, officials contemplated unleashing a strike force of homing pigeons armed with ampoules of anthrax against enemy targets, including the Kremlin. The plan, dating from the early days of the Cold War, turned out instead to be the last hurrah for pigeons in the British armed forces.

Carrier pigeons had performed hazardous missions in the Second World War. After being parachuted into occupied France, their chances of returning to England with vital information from the French resistance were rated at less than eight to one. The British anti-pigeon Falconry Unit arguably had a slightly better war record: 'whilst they never brought down an enemy bird, probably because there never were any,' one report noted, 'they did demonstrate that they could bring down any pigeon that crossed the area they were patrolling'.

In truth, radio and telephone had rendered the signals pigeon obsolete by mid-1945, and in the early days of peace the armed forces told Whitehall's Joint Intelligence Committee (JIC) that they would no longer pay for the maintenance of military pigeon lofts. This triggered a three-year argument within the JIC's Ad Hoc Committee on Carrier Pigeons over future 'pigeon policy'.

The birds' post-war champion was Wing Commander William Rayner MBE, head of the Air Ministry's pigeon section and author of a paper entitled 'The Future Uses of Pigeons'. Extrapolating from studies which suggested that the birds used electromagnetic fields and the Coriolis effect of the spinning earth to navigate, he asserted blithely that 'we can now train pigeons to "home" to any particular object on the ground when air released in the [enemy's] country', also confiding triumphantly that 'they are not detectable by radar'.

'All we need is a model of the small "target" and three weeks for special training by experts,' Rayner enthused. He mused that 'a thousand pigeons each with a 2oz explosive capsule landed at intervals on a specific target might be a seriously inconvenient surprise' for the enemy.

'Rayner has always been a menace in pigeon affairs,' fumed Colonel T.A. Robertson of MI5, whose own favourite, a Captain J. Caiger, was not immune to flights of fancy himself. His pigeon book promoted the 'secret of the eye', which stated that 'it was a proven fact' that the 'long distance racing qualities of pigeons depended to a large extent on the colour and make-up of their eyes'.

Some intelligence experts warned hawkishly that 'pigeon research will not stand still; if we do not experiment, other powers will'. So over the next few years new offensive uses were investigated, including training the birds to fly kamikaze missions into searchlights.

Committee members liaised with their American counterparts, who had a high-speed parachute system for dropping pigeons from planes. British academics were pestered to find out whether pigeons flew in a direct line or used the advantages of the terrain. Birds were released near an energy source at the Harwell research station to see if this disrupted their homing instincts, and pigeons and handlers alike were exposed to atomic radiation when a release was made from HMS *Arethusa*. The effects of atom bombs on pigeon efficiency bothered the committee greatly: were any pigeons experimented with at the H-bomb test at Bikini atoll in September 1948, they asked the Americans?

One observer bemoaned as early as 1945 that the committee of six was 'forced to swim in a sea of pigeon politics' and Caiger threatened to resign at one point. However, it was Rayner who blinked first in August 1947, after his request for a JIC typist to write up his manual on future pigeon uses was ignored.

The formerly secret pigeon files record correspondence with racing pigeon enthusiasts behind the Iron Curtain, Caiger's breeding experiments in his Surrey loft, and his pleas for more corn coupons to support a breeding programme based upon his 'secret of the eye'.

By 1948 even the JIC was becoming bored and 'invited' the Home Office to 'take over control of pigeons in war'. The HO seemed unenthusiastic and was still being chased by the JIC the following year. The neck of the subcommittee was finally wrung in 1950.

RATIONING THE OLYMPICS

After the Second World War, the renewal of the Olympic movement with its ideal of peaceful athletic competition was a symbolic priority. The Olympiad of 1936 had been hosted in Hitler's Berlin, and scheduled dates in 1940 and 1944 were abandoned owing to the conflict. In 1948, however, it was fitting that London should host the first post-war Games.

Clearly, austerity precluded anything on the scale of the triumphalist spectacular that Hitler had staged to promote the Aryan supremacy of pre-war Nazi Germany. One of the key problems to be overcome was simply how to feed the athletes and spectators. Nutritionally, the two Games could not have been more different. In 1936 the standard training diet consisted of multiple underdone steaks washed down with beer. But London in 1948 was firmly in the grip of food rationing, which would not finally disappear until bananas came off ration in 1954. This presented huge problems for the organizing committee and the different ministries involved.

The medical view was put forward by a young doctor called Magnus Pyke, who went on to become TV's first household-name medic with his trademark flailing arms. Pyke led the Accessory Food Factors Committee of the Medical Research Council, brought in to advise the organizing committee on nutrition issues. Pyke's group recommended that competing athletes should get what they wanted 'without restriction' until their events were over, while 'trainers, assistants and other supernumeraries should be restricted to the normal civilian ration'. This, would show the world the sacrifices that the nation was still making in the wake of the war.

This proposal was rejected by government officials, one of whom recorded that he 'need hardly point out that this is, in point of fact, administratively impossible'. Everyone was required to have a permit for their food, and the permits had to specify a limit. As the catering was subcontracted, permit-less arrangements would give 'a blank cheque' to the commercial caterers which, the writer implied, would test their honesty to the limit.

The result was a typical compromise. Athletes and assistants alike were allocated the 'Category A' daily allowance available for a worker in heavy industry, an arrangement that also allowed them to take supplementary meals which, an official pointed out, were quite substantial. This was boosted by an extra two pints of milk a day, plus a half pound of chocolates and sweets.

The organizing committee calculated that the daily calorie intake per athlete was just 3,900. No one was going to get fat on a diet built around daily allowances of 6 oz of meat, 2 oz of butter and fats, 1 oz of cheese and 1 oz of preserves. As Dr Pyke put it, when comparing 1948 with 1936, 'in those days the present weekly meat ration would have disappeared at one sitting'.

With the Games under way, the indefatigable Dr Pyke was involved in trying to measure the calorific input of various teams billeted around the capital. His female researchers met with a distinct lack of co-operation from the Australians and the Irish, while the analysis of the diet of the 140 Mexicans living in Preston Manor School in Wembley was hampered by a lack of data. 'It was difficult to obtain from the Spanish speaking chef an account of the ingredients used in his Mexican recipes,' the report drily notes.

Rations and food favouritism were key topics in press conferences before the Games opened, and Minister of Food, John Strachey, was briefed to point out that the extra rations provided during the eight weeks of the Games amounted to only 0.16 per cent of the nation's requirement. When the Americans complained that they needed fresh, rather than reconstituted, orange juice, the caterers told the organizing committee that they had explained that oranges were on ration but they could potentially find one a day per competitor. 'But, as we should have to take this quantity from the next distribution (which is intended, and is already earmarked, for domestic consumers) we could not make such an arrangement without the strongest possible cause.'

In the end, competitors were told they could bring whatever food they liked (free of import duties). A group of Americans spread around supplies of US army rations, and Iceland pitched in with a donation of a ton of frozen mutton. Dr Pyke was amazed when he found out that the Americans were flying in enriched white flour from Los Angeles on a daily basis. 'Other aspects of the catering are being done with a similar disregard for geography and expense,' he noted.

Chicken-powered nukes

In the early days of the Cold War British military contingency plans for the outbreak of a third world conflict involved the rapid retreat of land forces back across the Rhine from their German bases.

In the mid-1950s these plans called for the detonation of up to five 10-kiloton atomic land mines, code-named Blue Peacock, in a move designed to halt the Red Army in strategic locations by the Rhine. The weapons, each with a blast range of 20 miles, were designed to be buried as the onset of hostilities neared and then left behind during the westward retreat.

However, the scientists at Britain's top military research base at Aldermaston in Berkshire were confronted by an intractable problem. If the weapons were buried in the cold winter months, there was a risk that the delicate vital mechanisms might fail to work. What was needed was a means of keeping the insides of the seven-ton devices, each one the size of a small truck, warm enough to work faultlessly but without requiring a power source.

The answer to the problem is revealed almost as an aside in the Blue Peacock Project's Climatic Trial Test Report, dated October 1957. This recorded concern that the device did not perform well in the Arctic chamber test and could not meet the trial requirement of withstanding four consecutive days at a constant minus 25 degrees Fahrenheit.

The original paper from the Armament Research and Development Establishment is stamped 'Top Secret – Atomic, UK Eyes Only'. In Annexe A, which looked at heat-transfer characteristics and the usefulness of thermal insulation within the mine, recommendation number 21 on page 30 contained one of the strangest ideas in any nuclear-age document. It suggested that one means of improving the cold weather performance of the mine would be to increase the thickness of the insulation or to incorporate 'some form of heating independent of power supplies under the weapon hull in the emplacement'. It then went on to propose for the latter solution that 'chickens, with a heat output of the order of 1,000 B.T.U. per bird per day, are a possibility'.

Apparently, entombing a clutch of live chickens within the monster bomb with enough food to keep them alive for a few days would generate sufficient body heat to protect the mine's workings from the cold, without, one assumes, giving the increasingly hungry chickens long enough to work out a way to attack the mine's insides. Scientists reckoned the birds would last a week before they suffocated, starved or were atomized.

Mercifully, the mine, variations of which were code-named Blue Bunny and Big Bertha, appears never to have reached the War Office's operational requirement of −50 to 125 degrees Fahrenheit, and the project was cancelled in 1958. Had the mine been deployed, it was predicted that it would have killed everyone within a radius of 20 miles.

....

Road pricing: back to the 1970s

Proposals to use a tax on congestion to restrict traffic levels may sound thoroughly modern, but back in the early 1970s the Conservative Heath government was in favour of putting a 'black box' in every car to track its movements.

Yet even with the encouragement of the Treasury, which estimated at just £110 million the cost of implementing a national scheme, it did not take off.

The plan was binned by the Secretary of State for the Environment, who was 'not prepared to accept a technical experiment of road pricing, largely because the political reaction would be counter productive'.

While one official blithely claimed that congestion was the best deterrent against increasing car use, the documents from thirty-five years ago barely mention the environmental issues that preoccupy us today.

REDRAWING THE IRISH BORDER

In view of the centuries of effort that the English have expended on creating and maintaining a foothold in Ireland, it might seem unthinkable that as recently as three decades ago the British government appeared to contemplate, just for a moment, the transfer to the Irish Republic of large parts of the six counties of the province of Ulster in a bid to resolve the communal violence that erupted in Northern Ireland during the 1960s.

Yet a document once marked 'Top Secret' exists in the papers of the Office of the Prime Minister that suggests just that. Titled 'Redrawing the Border and Population Transfer', its remit was 'to consider whether it would be practicable to move the dissident Republican population out of Northern Ireland retaining only the Unionist population'. The tone of the paper, which dates from the Heath administration, indicates that the idea was not considered a serious proposition by the unnamed civil servant who drafted it, as he methodically raises a host of problems and faulty assumptions, any one of which would have rendered the plan almost inoperable. To modern eyes it reads like a paper that has been requested from on high and in the underlying premise of which the writer has no belief. Though the topic offers the opportunity to emulate the irony of Jonathan Swift's famous *A Modest Proposal* (in which Swift argued that the sufferings of the Irish nation could be reduced by allowing the rich to eat the babies of the poor), there is, alas, in this paper on Ireland not a trace of satire.

Playing a straight bat, the author begins by pointing out that, for the idea to have any chance of success, priority would have to be given to 'hiving off those areas with a simple Catholic majority at the most recent census'. That such a process might raise protests among most communities is alluded to in the qualifying observation that 'to conduct a fresh plebiscite for the purpose of obtaining the majority view in each area would be to invite delay and chaos in the areas concerned'.

The writer goes on to point out that 'such a scheme would have a number of flaws' and lists four key deal breakers:

'(i) It would create enclaves of Republican territory within Northern Ireland and Northern enclaves in the Republic.

(ii) It would transfer nearly as many Protestants as Catholics.

(iii) It would ignore the much larger Catholic population who live in local authority areas where they are not in the majority.

(iv) It would transfer some areas that are electorally Unionist.'

'About one third of the population of Northern Ireland would be on the move,' the author notes, before stating more obviously that 'such a massive movement would not be peacefully accomplished'. 'It is doubtful if the cohesive and large Catholic population of Belfast would agree to move,' he comments, pausing to add that it is difficult to conceive of a sure way of ascertaining the political views of a person who is unwilling to move according to the plan's preferences, and that in any case such a process of 'forced movement' would be contrary to European conventions.

Having poured cold water on the idea that a mass population transfer might 'be effectively carried out and permanently secured', he lands the final knockout punch: opposition in the Irish Republic would be 'vehement and universal'. 'Any reversal of the present policy of reconciliation, and the adoption of a policy of demarcation and compulsory ghettos, would emphasise in the crudest terms the present division of Ireland.' The political fallout, he writes, would be the downfall of the Lynch government in Dublin, a more hawkish replacement, appeals to the United Nations, etc., etc.

Just to be helpful, the document has two annexed maps that emphasize the impossibility of dividing the population.

The report even trips itself up over nomenclature, still in many ways a live sectarian issue, by crossing out references to 'the six counties' and 'the 26 counties' in favour of 'Northern Ireland' and 'the Republic'.

It is clear that the writer, though he never says it, thought the whole idea completely unworkable in practice and foolish in conception. One can only imagine that he was asked to draft it after a senior politician turned one day to his senior civil servant and asked irritably whether there was any way in which Britain could be shot of the whole problem of Northern Ireland by moving the Catholics into the Republic. Clearly not was the civil servant's reply.

••

Wilson's brewery brainwave

Dreaming up populist measures to increase Labour's chances of re-election in 1974, Harold Wilson devised the slogan 'Little Things That Mean a Lot'. He came up with eight ideas, including abolishing hare coursing and tackling the impact of juggernauts. But only one sounded like a winner: 'Protecting local breweries and saving the pint'.

Plan A was to nationalize small breweries to protect them from being taken over by major companies, Plan B to resist the impact of metrification so that the British pint of beer remained a simple pint.

Wilson won the election, but his resignation in 1976 marked the end of the road for post-war nationalization. Happily, though, thirty years on we still call a pint a pint.

39

Falklands offer to Ugandan Asians

When the Ugandan president, General Idi Amin, expelled nearly 50,000 Ugandans of Asian origin in 1972, the British government called on the chiefs of staff to implement an evacuation plan code-named Operation Argent.

Simultaneously, the Foreign Office asked the remaining colonies if they would take in some refugees. T.H. Layng, Colonial Secretary to the Executive Council in Stanley, capital of the Falkland Islands, reported back to the head of the FO's West Indian and South Atlantic section that the islanders, who suffered from a shortage of teachers, doctors and artisans, 'to my amazement … accepted this suggestion'.

'It would be wonderful to have a few Indian servants,' he followed up cheerily, noting that the salary of £30-50 per month would be supplemented 'with some perks' that he left unspecified.

Idi Amin's act ruined the Ugandan economy and he was ousted in 1979. The files do not record whether any refugees actually went to the Falklands in the end.

PROTECTING
THE NATION

"I'll tell nobody where anywhere is."

IRA spider plot fear

In the early days of the Second World War, when defeat by the Nazis appeared imminent, there were many fears circulating in the country. But none was quite as far-fetched as the IRA spider plot.

Metropolitan Police papers reveal a strongly worded letter written by one C. Rolfe in February 1940 to 'The Superintending Inspector, CID Branch, Scotland Yard'. The writer warned of the gravest consequences were the Black Widow spiders kept in London Zoo allowed to escape, and he urged the police to ensure that the zoo destroyed them all before the confusion of the Blitz allowed them to make a bid for freedom.

Mr Rolfe believed that such a sinister arachnid terrorist plot would appeal to the IRA. 'Bomb outrages having failed to frighten the British public, it is quite conceivable that other methods of a more subtle kind may be adopted. The escape of these huge, ugly and dangerous spiders would have, undoubtedly, a very unnerving effect upon the majority of people in this country, accustomed as they are to small harmless varieties. It is hardly likely that the glass case containing these insects would be bombed but it is possible that mischievous devilry might succeed in breaking the case to allow the insects to escape. These insects are, I understand, extremely prolific and breed with great rapidity. The puerile wishes of a few professors of insectology should not be allowed to endanger the national welfare,' he thundered, counselling that the only satisfactory safeguard was the complete elimination of the spiders. 'Otherwise the police authorities may have, possibly, the distasteful task of hunting for these loathsome insects before they have had a chance to breed.'

The Met file does not indicate whether a response was sent to Mr Rolfe or whether the arachnophiles in London Zoo increased their vigilance. Perhaps more startling for the modern reader is the fact that Mr Rolfe's wartime letter, postmarked Southampton 9.30 am, was later that same day received and read in London.

The real Dad's Army

On 14 May 1940 Anthony Eden, who had become Secretary of State for War just three days earlier, broadcast on the BBC a request for volunteers to join a nationwide local defence force.

A German invasion seemed inevitable until after the Battle of Britain was won by November 1940, and the enemy had made it clear that they considered volunteers as irregulars outside the protection of military conventions who were to expect little mercy. Yet within 24 hours 250,000 men, including many First World War veterans, had put down their names at local police stations.

Their task was to delay the invading German forces and so give regular army units time to regroup. As the risk of invasion receded, they took a key role in capturing shot-down German airmen, manning anti-aircraft batteries and carrying out bomb-disposal duties.

Eden had promised the volunteers that they would receive a uniform and be armed, but supplies were scarce. A public appeal for weapons brought in 20,000 firearms, including items from a London theatre's props room and the gun room at Sandringham. Many men were forced to parade and go on duty with an assortment of pick-axes, crowbars, coshes, spears, dummy rifles, pitchforks, broom handles, golf clubs, garden tools and even walking sticks. Hand weapons were often improvised, for example by clamping infantry bayonets to entrenching tool handles. The Home Guard pike, a length of drainpipe capped by a 17-inch bayonet, was highly unpopular. All in all, this motley collection of weapons helped fix the force's 'Dad's Army' image for ever.

Recognizing its importance for national morale, however, the Prime Minister took a close interest in the new force. Recently released Cabinet papers are peppered with Churchill's demands for information. On 18 June 1940 he asked for fortnightly statistics on men and rifles and posed one very basic question: 'from whom do they receive their orders?' Churchill's Chief of Staff, Major-General H.L. Ismay, was the recipient of many memos, often addressed using his nickname 'Pug'. The figures were not encouraging. By mid-July 1,166,212 men were registered but had been issued with only 226,830 rifles.

Churchill simply ploughed on. On 20 July Ismay informed Eden that the 'Prime Minister again reverted to the question of substituting the title Home Guard for the Local Defence Volunteers. He said that you agreed with him, and expressed the hope that the change would be made forthwith.' One senses some exasperation in Ismay's concluding comment: 'I expect that you already have this matter in hand, but I thought it right to let you know what the PM said.' Churchill was a stickler; when the next fortnightly return arrived, he personally crossed out 'Local Defence Force' in the title and initialled 'HG'.

Ismay wrote to Major-General Henry Pownall, Inspector-General of the Home Guard, with an idea for reducing time spent responding to Churchill's memos. A liaison officer, he suggested, will 'save a good deal of bothersome correspondence of this kind'. This officer was Captain Duncan

Sandys, a future Conservative minister married to Churchill's daughter Diana. His arrival backfired slightly, as Churchill's statistical demands increased.

Many Home Guard issues were decided at the most senior level. A rate of 3 shillings for 10 hours' continuous duty was agreed for the volunteers, the paucity of this sum covered by Churchill's injunction to call it 'sandwich money'. The PM was also worried that the Home Guard was being led by older officers brought out of retirement and urged the military to find some younger and more dynamic leaders. His fear is echoed in a letter from a New Zealand pensions expert called Noble Lowndes, writing from his home in Upper Warlingham, Surrey, who thought the Guard should be remodelled as commando units. 'Far too many officers in command think in terms of the last war,' he observed. 'It would be Gilbertian if it were not so serious.'

By the first week of August 1940 Churchill was tackling Ismay about uniforms. 'It is very important to get on with the uniforms for the Home Guard,' he memoed. 'Let me have a forecast of deliveries.' That week Home Guard numbers reached one-and-a-half-million men, but they had only 40,000 steel helmets and fewer than 550,000 rifles between them.

" NOW, LET ME SEE – DID THE INSTRUCTOR SAY 7 SECONDS OR 7 MINUTES ? "

As summer became autumn, the writer H.V. Morton wrote to the PM protesting that his Buckinghamshire unit had had its rifles taken away. Officials explained that the British rifles were needed by regular forces and were being replaced by .300 calibre American light-automatic rifles. However, by September only 12,000 of these had been made available, plus 50 rounds per man. Eighteen months later the problem had still not gone away. A report to Churchill in May 1942 notes that of the 306 million rounds of ammunition promised by the United States only 13 million had been received in Britain. This earned a curt note in the margin: 'it is astonishing that this was allowed to happen', initialled WSC. The last file note shows Churchill still chasing the ammunition.

More than 1,600 members of the Home Guard were killed on duty before the force was disbanded in 1945.

....

1911 census was MI5 spy tool

Census information has always been closed for 100 years, although geneologists continue to lobby for early access. However, Foreign Office minutes reveal that the 1911 census was released to the security services as early as 1913.

Sir Vernon Kell, Director-General of the Secret Service Bureau, from which MI5 emerged in 1916, reported that the census was proving of 'much help' in the task of registering aliens, particularly in the major cities. It is likely that the lists created from it assisted greatly when it came to arresting aliens at the outbreak of the First World War.

HITLER FOR DEATH CHAIR, SAID CHURCHILL

As the Second World War turned slowly in the Allies' favour, the British government began to focus its attention on deciding how to deal with captured leaders of the Axis powers.

Prime Minister Winston Churchill was ready in 1942 to declare them outlaws and summarily execute them to avoid the complications of a formal trial. War Cabinet notes record him saying: 'Contemplate that if Hitler falls into our hands we shall certainly put him to death.' On 6 July 1942 he saw Hitler as a leader who was not a sovereign and therefore could not hide behind his government and blame his ministers, as Germany's Kaiser Wilhelm had done in the previous war. 'This man is the mainspring of evil,' the note taker has Churchill observing. One can imagine the Prime Minister chewing on his cigar as he continues: 'Instrument – electric chair, for gangsters no doubt available on Lease Lend.'

The comments are contained in notes made by Sir Norman Brook, deputy cabinet secretary between 1942 and 1945, which are being transcribed and made available online on the National Archives' website.

During the following two years the British attempted to persuade the Allies that a trial was a mistake, but with little success. Churchill's opposition to a public trial was built on his assessment of the English Civil Wars, during which parliamentarian leaders put King Charles I on trial as a tyrant prior to beheading him, in the process creating a highly visible martyr.

Allied support for summary action was not forthcoming. The United States disagreed on principle, and the Russian leader Joseph Stalin knew that show trials could be very useful. From this shaky start, at their trials in Nuremberg the Nazi leaders found themselves as guinea-pigs for a new concept, that of international criminal law. The top-ranking Nazi official, Hermann Goering, and his co-defendants originally refused to participate, but in the end they became caught up in the drama and took part in the procedures. The same dilemmas have beset the public trial of deposed Iraqi leader Saddam Hussein.

Back in March 1945 the War Cabinet was concerned about deportation issues. On 12 April 1945, the day President Roosevelt died, they considered the issue of war crimes again. Churchill was in favour of a Bill of Attainder, a device that allowed the British parliament to condemn someone who had fallen out of political favour without a trial. The Cabinet agreed that the idea of a mock trial was objectionable: better to view the executions as political and be direct about it.

Churchill believed that 'the trial will be a farce. Indictment: facilities for counsel. All sorts of complications ensue as soon as you admit a fair trial. I agree with H.O. [Home Office]: tht they shd be treated as outlaws. We shd however seek agreemt. of our Allies.' Churchill was adamant that he would 'take no responsibility for a trial – even tho' the U.S. want to do it'.

On 3 May 1945 the Cabinet examined the situation again, as both Hitler and Mussolini were now dead. Churchill speculated whether Britain could negotiate a peace settlement with Himmler 'and bump him off later', another strategy that had Home Office agreement. That the territory was uncharted is revealed in the range of comments on the issue. One official recorded that 'Buchenwald is not a <u>war</u> crime', a technicality that earned a terse aside from Churchill: 'don't quibble'.

In the end, the PM decided to give way to the Russians and the Americans, who were still pushing for trials; the US had also flirted with the idea of a mass denazification plan. 'Don't make a big fight with U.S. & R. on this. We are in weak pos^n.' Churchill was inclined to be pragmatic now that so many of the top leaders had been removed from the equation, but he still held firmly to the view that the 'fewer trials the better'.

By 30 May 1945 Eden had recognized that the Americans 'have come up a long way to meet us. No dispos^n for grand trials.' The solution was an Allied court for major criminals hemmed in by procedures designed to prevent those indicted from using it as a platform. By then 167 prisoners were awaiting attention, including former deputy leader of the Nazi party Rudolf Hess, who had flown to England in 1941. Churchill warned that public opinion might go against the process 'if the numbers are large', and others counselled, speed or otherwise, the trials would 'make us look ridiculous'.

The Nuremberg trials began on 20 November 1945 and ran until 13 April 1949. Their articles specified that they were to review crimes against peace, war crimes and crimes against humanity, and that neither the possession of an official position nor having a superior would prevent an individual from being tried. Their impact on international law still reverberates today.

●●

Operation Unthinkable

There is a dossier in the National Archives with the stark title 'Russian Threat to Western Civilization'. The plan, later known as Operation Unthinkable, was drawn up by the Joint Planning Staff in May 1945. It speculated how force might be used to 'impose upon Russia the will of the United States and the British Empire' and set 1 July 1945 as the date for commencing hostilities.

Churchill was afraid that a swift withdrawal of US forces from Europe would leave Britain vulnerable to a Russian advance as well as result in the loss of Persian and Iraqi oilfields.

The paper believed that it would take 'total war' to inflict defeat on Russia in the field, where it had a three to one manpower advantage.

Operation Unthinkable was never developed into a coherent plan. By 1946 it was clear that US troops would be based in Europe for a long time.

Ice cream & D-Day

When Allied troops hit the Normandy beaches on D-Day, 6 June 1944, the commanders of Operation Overlord had two advantages that their Nazi enemies knew nothing about. Both had taken years of planning and were instrumental in the success of the invasion.

The first was a detailed project to lay fuel pipelines on two routes from England to France that would support the Allied invasion by replacing the need for hundreds of vulnerable tanker crossings. The second was a set of battle maps of the German coastal defences around the five invasion beaches, drawn up largely using details culled from millions of pre-war British holiday snaps.

Many technical innovations were employed during the invasion, including the successful Mulberry harbours for disembarking troops and materiel, though there were also some costly failures. The biggest stroke of all was PLUTO (the PipeLine Under The Ocean), which supplied fuel to northern France along two routes originating in Dungeness in Kent and the Isle of Wight in Hampshire.

The success of the 715,000-strong invasion force depended on an uninterrupted fuel supply. Secret preparations for PLUTO on the British side started more than a year before the invasion took place. Fuel was stored away from areas the Luftwaffe might be monitoring and moved by pipeline from Bristol and Liverpool to the PLUTO pipeline heads on the south coast. Two types of experimental undersea pipe, which required huge amounts of lead and steel, were designed using submarine cable technology. Ironically, one of the main manufacturers was called Siemens Brothers of Woolwich, though so much piping was needed that almost one-fifth of the length had to be made in the USA.

The fuel supply network was carefully disguised so as not to attract German attention. Parts of it, including pumping stations and access points, were rigged out as civilian buildings such as ice cream parlours, garages and bungalows. The National Archives recently released a collection of photographs of the construction work associated with the PLUTO project. These show things ranging from a row of disguised villas at Dungeness, which hid several pump houses, to a 1,200-ton floating cable-laying drum, nicknamed a 'conun' (an abbreviation of a fictitious HMS *Conundrum*), being hauled across the Channel.

During its lifetime the pipeline, which was some 710 miles long, supplied 172 million gallons of fuel. Though its dimensions must have been known to thousands, it wasn't until May 1945 that a publisher challenged the D-Notice the government had slapped on all talk about fuel supplies to the invasion force. Churchill simply noted in the margin of the memo alerting him of the impending publication: 'I think this is all right now.'

The Overlord beach maps, code-named Bigot, that were relied on during the invasion were meticulously created using intelligence brought in by dangerous clandestine reconnaissance operations and supplied in ignorance by the British public. Back in May 1942 the

Admiralty had appealed over the BBC Home Service for listeners to dig out their holiday snaps and postcards from abroad during 'the carefree days of peace' and send them in for intelligence use. Over five million items were eventually donated, many of them filtering by mid-1943 into the initial planning for the invasion of Europe which was then under way in great secrecy.

Fortunately, the Normandy coastline and particularly the five landing beaches had been popular pre-war holiday destinations for Britons, especially the key seaside resorts of Ouistreham, Arromanches and Courseulles. Details gleaned from the many Normandy items were fed into a mapping project put together in dozens of secret locations, including inside Selfridges department store in London. The output gave the invading Allied forces the excellent start they needed, as they made a beachhead in continental Europe and began the march on Berlin.

"As you see, Peabody, your old job is still waiting for you."

Prison camps at Ascot, Epsom and Butlins

One of the stranger outcomes of Cold War anxiety was the Labour government's top-secret plan to detain communists at British pleasure sites if war broke out with the Soviet Union.

MI5 files running from 1948 to 1954 reveal that the Home Office proposed to corral potential troublemakers within 48 hours of 'M day' (mobilization day). All officials agreed there was a 'need for action before legislation in arrest and the conduct of searches'. MI5 would supply names from their aptly titled Everest List; by one estimate 3,000 aliens and British subjects were considered a risk.

An obvious snag was that, for reasons including 'grave political embarrassment', the Home Office could not be seen to set up prisons from scratch without public explanation. Suggestions for sites that could be requisitioned in an emergency included the Butlins holiday camp at Prestatyn and, as an interrogation centre, the London Oratory, today better known as Tony Blair's controversial choice for his sons' schooling. By 1950 Ascot, Epsom and a holiday camp near Rhyl

55

had been earmarked as holding camps and two Isle of Man holiday camps as suitable for lengthier detentions.

None of the officials involved seems to have savoured the irony of the sites' change in function or to have indulged in speculation about how the detainees – some of whom would be arrested on omnibus orders with little explanation – might feel on finding sand or turf beneath their feet.

Planning rumbled on for years. Some of the camp requirements were quickly agreed, such as the need to segregate aliens from home-grown communists, whom MI5 feared might be 'barrack lawyers' inclined to incite their foreign companions to appeal against their detention.

Other details caused bickering. MI5 officials had concerns that a camp commandant hostile to their presence might be hired from the ranks of the police. The War Office, having deflected Home Office attempts to lay the whole plan at its door, was prepared to supply security devices such as searchlights and minefields but initially drew the line at the provision of barbed wire. It was also wary of the communists. A Major Birley wished to establish 'the type of person likely to be involved' and posed the key question: 'Are they likely to be "dangerous" and make every effort to get away, or will they be fairly docile and easy to handle?'

By 1954 some essentials had been at least loosely nailed down. The plan would be activated by a secret message to senior officials: 'HILLARY ESTABLISH

CAMPS', to be followed by immediate arrests. While the army guarded the camp perimeters, the police would provide internal discipline, grimly aware of the 'highly undesirable' characters involved and the risk of violence and even rioting. Other staff would come from the Home Office, the prison service and the Ministry of Works. MI5 spies would pose as welfare officers in order to mingle with the detainees and would have prior access to the sites to install bugging devices, or what they discreetly termed 'certain equipment'.

Predictably, the Women's Voluntary Service (WVS) was enlisted for kitchen duties as it was felt that while the Geneva Convention allowed alien internees to do domestic chores, British prisoners might refuse to cook their own suppers. It was hoped that 'any recalcitrant British subjects would soon decide that it was worth working to provide for their own comfort', but at a final top-level meeting Colonel St Johnson, the Chief Constable of Lancashire, remained gallantly concerned about the 'unfair burden' on the WVS.

Proposals ultimately got bogged down in indecision and red tape. Five and a half years after the need for immediate action had been agreed, the plan remained full of holes, such as the Ministry of Works' insistence that no matter how urgently the camps were required, it could not provision them without two weeks' notice. The final document in the file promises only further debate and careful study of 'such points as appeared to be outstanding'.

STRING VESTS AND SUEZ

As the sense of crisis deepened in the Middle East during 1956, one British defence official was beavering away on a piece of research with potentially huge implications for the deployment of British troops in hot climates. Even as the government lurched towards the launch of the Anglo-French invasion of the Canal Zone, in what history now describes as the Suez crisis, Mr K.W.L. Kenchington seized the hour to publish his masterwork: a detailed account of the effectiveness of kit item CM0231, the army's regulation string vest.

This was a pressing matter within the Directorate of Physiological and Biological Research of the Clothing and Stores Experimental Establishment in the Ministry of Supply, which was concerned that no serious study had been conducted into the undergarment's usefulness to troops serving in hot climates. The assiduous Mr Kenchington was detailed to carry out such a study, spending July and August 1955 testing two additional types of string vest on troops billeted, with Egypt's agreement, in the Suez Canal Zone. Twenty-four men of the 1st Battalion the Royal Warwicks were ordered to don one of the three vests being assessed in temperatures of up to 98 degrees Fahrenheit for periods of up to nine days. Pitted against the standard British army string vest (the CM0231) were the standard cotton singlet (the CC1821) and a new wider-mesh vest made by Courtaulds under the code name Sherpa. 'All vests were washed together, at intervals of three days, by the same dhobie,' the report notes scientifically.

Stimulated by the apparent growth in the number of string-vest adherents in the summer months in Britain, the report set out to fathom subjectively their benefits in hot climates. Mr Kenchington, clearly a thorough man, spent more than a year analysing the results before passing them on to Whitehall, the Suez crisis deepening all the while. A masterpiece of qualitative assessment backed up by statistical data, the report details the degrees of 'coolness, sweatiness, drag, chafing, impression, bulkiness … and ease of donning and doffing'. While coming down firmly in favour of the Sherpa vest, which proved particularly popular among habitual vest wearers working in kitchens, the real surprise for the authors was the discovery that more than 60 per cent of participants did not usually wear a vest at all, as 'it was understood in advance of the trial that the number of men in the Canal Zone who did not wear a vest was negligible'.

Expanding the study to 69 men, the authors were perplexed that only two non-wearers were 'converted' to vest use by the experiments. In their recommendations they noted sternly that 'in view of the resistance to any vest by subjects accustomed to doing without, efficient indoctrination and a generous period of experience are important in any future assessment' (which translated means 'it's good for them and they should get used to it').

External events, however, were working against the long-term wearing of any Forces vest, certainly in Egypt. The British and French governments were opposed to any Egyptian takeover of the Suez Canal, which threatened to lengthen the sea voyage to their vital Middle Eastern oil suppliers and their Far Eastern colonies. Three months after Egypt's president, Gamal Abdel Nasser, nationalized the canal in July 1956, Israeli forces invaded Gaza and Sinai in concert with the British and French, who promptly sent their forces to keep the canal open. Militarily this was feasible, but politically it was a huge mistake. Within sight of their objective, British and French forces were forced, under United Nations, US and Russian pressure, to withdraw.

The British Prime Minister, Anthony Eden, left office a broken man. Suez became the first international crisis where UN peacekeeping troops were deployed. The canal itself remained closed to maintain the ceasefire until 1975.

WO 352/58

SPIES AROUND EVERY CORNER

The orientalist and Bram Stoker's 'Dracula'

Rarely do the files underplay the colourful nature of their subject more than in the case of the Central European Orientalist Armin Vambery.

As a young man Vambery had travelled through Central Asia disguised as a dervish, before in his thirties taking up a professorship in oriental languages at the university in Budapest, a post he held until his death nearly half a century later. The post clearly didn't pay very well, so, being short of money, the professor, like a kind of latter-day Casanova, embarked upon regular tours of Europe's capitals, trading upon the reputation founded on his arcane knowledge to charm his way into high society.

Armed with a letter of introduction to the Prime Minister, Lord Palmerston, he attempted to make himself indispensable to the British government by passing on titbits of intelligence gleaned from non-English-speaking oriental leaders such as the Sultan of Turkey. As early as 1873 he was feeding London stories of Russian plots in Central Asia, part of the 'Great Game' the British engaged in to thwart Russia's designs upon British India.

In 1875 Vambery wrote to the Foreign Office from

Budapest pointing out that his articles in the Austro-Hungarian press had consistently advanced British interests and asking for money, as he was unable to make ends meet from his literary efforts. Senior Foreign Office officials were dunned into making a series of large ex-gratia payments, generally described as 'contributions for travelling expenses', over many years before Vambery approached King Edward VII and was successful in securing an annual pension.

The file contains letters to Vambery from his Foreign Office paymasters which he 'voluntarily surrendered' to the government in 1911, two years before his death. Sadly, none of his letters to them, or letters to him from his many admirers in Britain, including Queen Victoria, have survived.

To modern readers Vambery's chief claim to fame is the mention by the vampire hunter van Helsing in Bram Stoker's novel *Dracula* of 'my friend Arminius from Buda-Pesth university'. One of Stoker's biographers claimed that it was Vambery who introduced Stoker to the Dracula legend during a dinner of the legendary Beefsteak Club in 1890, hosted by the actor-manager Sir Henry Irving and held in the back rooms of the Lyceum Theatre in London, where Stoker was the business manager. Other more prosaic accounts suggest that Stoker read of the vampire legend in a book borrowed from the public library in Whitby where he was on holiday and merely traded upon Vambery's reputation by citing his name.

Spies' guide to London

Soviet spies coming to London in the late 1930s had access to a detailed guide to the pre-war British capital that offered tips on where to meet a fellow agent, social etiquette, and how to avoid the attention of the police.

British intelligence found the documents at the end of the Second World War in the files of the German military intelligence agency, the Abwehr, in Brussels. The Germans had received them from Paris, where they had been found under the floorboards in the flat of Henri Robinson, a leading Soviet spy. Fluent in Russian, German, French and English, Robinson carried an array of passports under various names. His real identity remains unconfirmed.

The origins of the guide are unclear, but Robinson may have compiled it alongside Leopold Trepper, one of the Soviet Union's most effective spies, who went on to run the highly successful Red Orchestra spy ring (Die Rote Kapelle) in Nazi-occupied France. He is known to have visited England five or six times in the period 1937–9, when the guide was being put together.

The document gives advice on how best to keep a low profile and pass unnoticed in public. On arriving in

London, it cautions, one can stay for a few days in the best hotels, such as the Dorchester and the Ritz, but for longer stays a serviced flat is the preferred option. Police control, rare in hotels, is most unlikely outside them and the spy can therefore work unfettered. Nonetheless, 'it is advisable to arrive in all hotels with smart and sufficient luggage – the British spend a lot of money on good luggage and travellers risk being turned away or asked for a deposit if they do not comply with this custom'.

A topnotch address, such as Kensington, deflects suspicion, though the guide counsels that any rendezvous should be arranged in an outlying borough, where police numbers are much lower than in the city centre.

Working spies will find plenty of opportunities to check whether they are being followed by nipping in and out of the big department stores and major museums, for example the Science Museum, which have many exits.

A diverse range of meeting places is recommended, from the tunnels under Piccadilly Circus, to the statue of Peter Pan in Kensington Gardens, the Old Oak tearooms in Pinner and outside Wimbledon post office. For important meetings the guide suggests a quick train ride to Oxford or Cambridge, doubtless ideal places for people with foreign accents to meet in public.

The top tip was to take out membership of the Automobile Association at two guineas a year. This could turn out to be an excellent investment as the AA offered free legal representation in the courts for members, thus keeping the spy away from the close attention of the police in the event of a traffic accident.

REAL BOND ANTICS

The writer Ian Fleming, it is speculated, based James Bond on real life. Fleming worked in naval intelligence during the Second World War and among the papers that crossed his desk were some from Gibraltar, the British outpost off southern Spain. Files recently released include details of daring Italian underwater sabotage operations against shipping anchored by the Rock that Fleming later mimicked in *Thunderball*.

Acquired from Spain in 1704, Gibraltar's two square miles were riddled with tunnels containing war materiel and a prime naval dockyard. While no full-scale attack on the colony ever took place during the war, spies could sit in comfort in neutral Spain and, using only binoculars, monitor every ditch and adit, read the call sign of every plane, watch every ship unload and each convoy steam out of the bay. And with thousands of Spanish workers walking daily across the airfield to work in the colony, the port was rife with contraband and gossip.

'Sabotage on the Rock was in fact much easier to advance, even at the end of the war, than enemy agents appeared to think. We had to rely on hoodwinking them, not having any other adequate defence,' noted Major David Scherr, head of the Defence Security Office (DSO). One tactic was to take the fight to the enemy by penetrating their organizations, a strategy so successful that the DSO was obliged to fake examples of sabotage to help its double agents establish their credibility.

The DSO's main concern was Giulio Pistono, the Italian leader of an underwater sabotage team targeting British and Allied shipping in the bay, who lived in a villa in Spain. Between 1940 and 1944 the Italians made seven underwater sabotage attempts, five of which were successful and destroyed 14 ships. The attacks were mounted by manned torpedoes operating ten metres below the surface. The frogmen would submerge 100 metres before the target to attach bombs to ships' hulls.

It is likely that Fleming read the story of the divers of the 10th Flotilla MAS who manoeuvred a damaged tanker, the *Olterra*, into Algeciras harbour. Over several months they cut away the forward bulkhead and installed a torpedo rack, creating a clandestine underwater launch pad that was never detected by Scherr's men. Fortunately, a major Italian underwater assault in December 1942, which targeted three capital ships including the aircraft carriers *Furious* and *Formidable*, was repulsed by the Allies.

Sherr's lengthy report contains many exotic details Fleming may well have stored away for the future, including the description of a prototype Bond girl – 'a rather seedy but not unattractive imitation of the seductive female spy of the thrillerette type' – who introduced herself as 'the Queen of Hearts'. Used by Scherr as a spy, her cook's brother saw some frogmen leaving on a raid from a Spanish beach, information which ultimately led Scherr to unravel the Italian operation. His report also mentions an exploding fountain pen and describes, with exasperation, how it was discovered at the end of the war that Pistono's rented villa was actually owned by a Briton.

Sir Hardy Amies given dressing-down

Senior officers in the British special forces were not quite sure what to make of Hardy Amies. Bilingual in German and a fluent French speaker, his language skills had seen him selected to join the Intelligence Corps in 1941.

'More of a soldier in performance than his looks', noted Lieutenant Colonel R.E. Brooks in an early report. 'Far tougher both physically and mentally than his rather precious appearance would suggest,' concluded the head of the Special Operations Executive, Major General Collin Gubbins, some years later.

The SOE had been set up by Churchill 'to set Europe ablaze' through subversion and sabotage. Its agents were often parachuted in behind enemy lines and faced capture and execution by the Nazis. Precious or not, Amies joined the SOE's Belgian Section in 1943 and became known for using the names of fashion accessories as code words. In February 1944 he became its head.

The Belgian Section lost 105 of 258 agents in the field, partly due to treachery by Belgian collaborators as well as German infiltration and successful counter-intelligence. So in late 1944 the last thing senior SOE officials wanted was to run risks that might expose their operatives to further danger. They were thus perturbed to learn that Lieutenant Colonel Amies had set up a photo shoot for *Vogue* in newly liberated Brussels, complete with pictures and descriptions of SOE agents.

Intelligence officers paid a visit to Audrey Withers, the 'editress' of the British *Vogue* (known to insiders as *Brogue*), and were shocked to read an article that colourfully described the 'baby face' of the young Countess d'Urssel as 'a perfect passport for her activities in the resistance movement. She is supposed to have carried millions of francs in her handbag.' Miss Withers complied with requests for changes but pointed out that Amies' reason for visiting Belgium, to hand out medals to Belgian spies, was plastered all over the local press.

An officer initialled in the report as 'J. R.' confined himself to removing details of Amies' wartime career but wrote to his superiors that it seemed extraordinary to him that 'a serving officer should lend himself and his Secret-Service background in the interests of his private affairs, to wit, one of England's chief dress designers employed by the House of Worth to a gaudy publicity stunt … no doubt the profile of Lt Col Amies in the next issue of Vogue will cause a flutter in many feminine hearts when they realise that their handsome couturier is, after all, the "Scarlet Pimpernel" of this war.'

As *The Times* noted on his death in 2003, Amies was more of a pink pimpernel than a red one, a fact either well disguised from his superiors during the war or simply ignored. Amies enjoyed huge success as a designer after the war, supplying outfits to the present queen from 1950. 'Not bad for a suburban frock maker,' he once said.

The scientist super-spy

Klaus Fuchs was the most important scientist to be tried and imprisoned as a Cold War Soviet spy, and the National Archives holds no fewer than 26 secret-service files on him.

In 1933 Fuchs fled Nazi Germany to England via France. At the start of the Second World War he was interned and shipped to Canada before his excellent reputation led the Royal Society to petition for his return. By 1942 he was working with Professor Rudolf Peierls, a fellow German refugee, who had co-authored the short paper that first outlined how an atomic bomb could be constructed using Uranium-235. The files note that Fuchs lived at the professor's home while in Birmingham, paying £2 a week rent.

In 1944 Fuchs worked in New York with the British Atomic Energy Mission. In August of that year he transferred to Los Alamos, the secret heart of the Manhattan project (the US plan to build an atomic bomb), where he remained until mid-1946. After that he was employed at Britain's atomic research institute in Harwell until 1950, when he was interrogated by MI5 and confessed.

A leading theoretical physicist, Fuchs produced many of the calculations relating to the first atomic weapons, while his work on the much more powerful hydrogen bomb anticipated the solution that was eventually used. Even without his spying career he would have earned a prominent place in the history of the bomb; with it his place became unique.

Under interrogation he quickly revealed details of his Soviet links, apparently in the naive hope that he could continue to work at Harwell. After the Nazis invaded the Soviet Union in 1941, he started passing secrets to the Russians in the belief that they should have the knowledge that the Western Allies had discovered. Among the key data he passed on were details about the fundamental principles of isotope separation, the development of the plutonium bomb, and the results of the first atomic bomb test, code-named Trinity, in New Mexico in July 1945. Looking back, everyone wondered how it had been possible for a Soviet spy to have worked for so long at the heart of these secret programmes.

Fuchs in fact had convincing credentials. The British knew that he'd been accused by the Gestapo of being a communist in the run-up to the war, but they interpreted this as a positive sign of his anti-Nazi views rather than as a long-term threat. At his trial his defence counsel stated that it was known that he consorted with communists while in the UK, but his views had been glossed as almost apolitical. The files show that he passed no fewer than six security reviews, while a January 1948 assessment concluded: 'we think that the security risk is very slight'. He was only investigated after a request was received from the FBI in August 1949.

The fact is that Fuchs's war work was so valuable to the Allies that the desire for his input overcame any concerns about the risks associated with his gaining wider knowledge. In effect, a calculated risk was taken, and the calculation was then forgotten.

Fuchs received a sentence of fourteen years. Released after nine years, he moved to East Germany, where he had a distinguished academic career and a seat on the Communist Party's Central Committee.

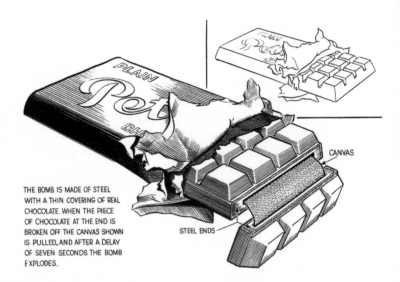

THE BOMB IS MADE OF STEEL WITH A THIN COVERING OF REAL CHOCOLATE. WHEN THE PIECE OF CHOCOLATE AT THE END IS BROKEN OFF THE CANVAS SHOWN IS PULLED, AND AFTER A DELAY OF SEVEN SECONDS THE BOMB EXPLODES.

CANVAS

STEEL ENDS

Exploding chocolate

Deep in the files there is a set of papers that record the different forms of camouflage used by German forces in the Second World War to disguise their sabotage equipment. Each one of the detonators, explosives and incendiary devices in this extraordinary catalogue was taken from a captured German agent.

Early in the war the disguises were often prosaic: a canteen of tea, a thermos flask or a tin of peas. As the war progressed, however, the ideas became more imaginative. Hiding a bomb in a lump of coal might conceal it well providing there were other lumps around it, but woe betide the agent who forgot which one contained the explosive material.

In many cases the device was camouflaged as a friendly English-labelled product such as Smedley's Dessert English Red Plums or Ovaltine, or as an everyday object such as a bar of soap or an oilcan.

But among the booby-trapped attaché cases and the modified throat pastilles that doubled as incendiary devices, one piece of equipment stands out for its imaginative ingenuity: the hand grenade disguised as a bar of Peter's chocolate. Break off the end of the bar and a canvas strap is revealed that invites the holder to pull it and activate the grenade's timer. The holder then had seven seconds to ditch the bar before it exploded.

This particular device was found on a spy named Jan Marie Lallart in April 1943, after he had been landed by German submarine on the North African coast near Port Etienne in Mauritania. On surrendering to the French, he was passed to the British for a month for interrogation, a note in his file hinting darkly that the French wanted him back as they were likely to execute him as a traitor.

One wonders how practical this grenade would have been. The steel device was covered by a very thin layer of chocolate that would surely have melted very quickly in a hot climate. The unknown brand might have been a giveaway in an English-speaking country too.

German ingenuity in designing such devices was, as in the Lallart case, not matched by their efficiency in delivering them. It is believed that British intelligence identified every single German agent that landed on British soil during the Second World War, and only one is thought possibly to have escaped capture. This seems hardly surprising given the ineptitude of the three spies who were landed in neutral southern Ireland in 1940 carrying a bomb disguised as a tin of French peas. In a fit of misplaced optimism about the depth of Irish nationalism and the readiness of the population to rise up against the British, they asked the first person they met to take them to the IRA, only to be led instead rather tamely to the local police station.

UGLY COUNT WAS THE ENGLISH PATIENT

Hollywood is famous for providing a positive gloss on dubious characters, but none more so in recent times than the hero of *The English Patient*, the Hungarian count Laszlo Almasy, played with aplomb in the 1996 film by Ralph Fiennes.

In Anthony Minghella's film the count is a handsome map-maker in British employ, a tragic character who suffers horrible burns in a plane crash in the Sahara and whose life is blighted by lost love for the English wife of a fellow explorer. The picture that emerges from the files of the Secret Intelligence Service (SIS) could not be more different. The security services' report described the German spy 'Count' Almasy as 'very thin, tall, prominent nose, spectacles, brown hair, very ugly with nervous tic'. The renowned desert explorer was also a hopeless spymaster, the report concluded.

Almasy was apparently recruited by German intelligence when he was ordered by the British to leave Egypt at the outbreak of the Second World War. Sent to work for General Rommel's Afrika Korps, he was tasked with infiltrating agents into the Egyptian capital, Cairo, to collect information on British troop movements. At this early stage of the war the battle for North Africa hung in the balance.

The files relate the story of some of Almasy's failed escapades through the debriefings of his captured spies.

The most famous took place in May 1942 when he drove two agents named Eppler and Sandstede across the Libyan desert to Cairo. Following tracks that Almasy had used to explore the desert back in 1932, by the time the spies arrived their mission had already become hopeless as the German army wireless contact they were to report to had been captured by Allied forces.

On reaching the Egyptian capital, the spies sought a discreet place to hide whilst they found somewhere to locate their wireless transmitter. Their choice of a brothel was not, perhaps, inspired, but the pair compounded this by going on a spending spree in the city's nightclubs during which they tried to milk British officers for information. They were also carrying large quantities of sterling, which was not valid in Egypt and the possession of which was an imprisonable offence.

Within two months, spent largely it seems at the Kit Kat Club, their behaviour had blown their cover and led to their arrest. 'They achieved nothing, as far as can be discovered,' MI5's report concludes. 'They were unable or unwilling to make certain contacts which they had been told to make and because they were too much intoxicated with the possession of so much money and too intent upon enjoying the flesh pots of Egypt in the form of women and wine.'

One quaint touch is that Almasy used English novels to provide the keys to encode his wireless messages.

Almasy returned to his native Hungary after the war, where he was arrested. Following months of interrogation, he was eventually released and died in 1952.

The Indian spy princess

Noor Inayat-Khan's history is both complex and simple. A descendant of Tipu Sultan, the Tiger of Mysore, she was born in Moscow and brought up in Paris, where she studied music with Nadia Boulanger for a while and became a writer of children's tales. An Indian Muslim and a Sufi, she was a pacifist by conviction. A firm believer in Indian independence, she took the principled decision to escape from occupied France and reach Britain, the colonial oppressor, in order to fight the tyranny of Nazism.

Once in England she joined the WAAF, before being picked out for intelligence work owing to her fluency in French. As a Special Operations Executive wireless operator in occupied Paris in 1943 she outwitted the Nazis for months before she was caught. She is also, by a country mile, the bravest person mentioned in this book. An hour spent thumbing through her SOE file is both humbling and chilling.

Inayat-Khan's training reports suggest that she was not especially cut out for intelligence work. 'Clumsy and slow: no aptitude for PT,' notes one; 'pretty scared of weapons,' notes another; 'no use at field sketches,' concludes a third. In March 1943 a Major de Wesselow commented that Noor 'hadn't the foggiest idea what the training was going to be about' and that she had confessed she would not like to do anything 'two-faced' by 'deliberately cultivating friendly relations with malice aforethought'.

But her perseverance, including voluntary PT sessions, impressed her superior. In his final report a Major Wilkinson commented that she was 'not over-burdened with brains', a comment underlined by Maurice Buckmaster, head of F Section covering France, and tersely annotated: 'we don't want them over-burdened with brains'. Major Wilkinson's view was that Noor had 'an unstable and temperamental personality and it is very doubtful whether she is really suited for work in the field', an assessment which earned from Buckmaster the withering: 'Nonsense. Makes me cross.'

Buckmaster was clearly the more prescient. When an emergency wireless operator task in France was required at short notice in June 1943, it was Noor who was landed in a tiny Lysander aircraft by moonlight. Code-named Madeleine, she was instructed to link up with a spy network in Paris and transmit details of troop movements back to London. Women did not stand out as much as men in occupied territory, but they had to carry around a heavy radio in a suitcase and frequently move location. The network was quickly compromised but Noor refused to return to London, becoming virtually the last link between the resistance in Paris and the SOE in London.

In October the Gestapo finally caught up with her. Despite undergoing a month of interrogation, and knowing that the Germans had her code book and record of transmissions, she refused to reveal anything more. After attempting to escape, she was transferred to a prison at Pforzheim and held for 10 months in solitary confinement, in chains and on the lowest rations. She was then transported to the concentration camp at Dachau, just outside Munich, where she was viciously beaten and shot soon after her arrival.

Her SOE file reveals that for a long time the agency did not know what had happened to her. At first they thought she had been executed in July 1944 in Natzweiler prison. When they did find out the truth, the letter to the next of kin omitted any details of how she had died, saying that Noor, and three other executed female spies, had all last been seen 'in good spirits and good health' before their deaths.

SOE was formally disbanded in 1946, but Inayat-Khan's recommendation for the George Cross, the highest British award for bravery outside of the battlefield, was accepted in 1949.

Assistant Section Officer Noor Inayat-Khan is one of only three wartime female holders of the George Cross. The other two were SOE colleagues: Ensign Violette Szabo and Lieutenant Odette Sansom.

AMBASSADOR'S VALET SOLD D-DAY SECRETS

One of the most notorious intelligence lapses of the Second World War took place in neutral Ankara inside the home of the British ambassador, the splendidly named Old Etonian Sir Hughe Knatchbull-Hugesson.

British security services began to suspect that there was a leak inside the embassy in 1941 after a tip-off from the Soviets. The suspect, the ambassador's Yugoslavian butler, remained employed until April 1943, as Sir Hughe claimed that it 'had not been practical' to dismiss him until a successor could be found. Alas for Sir Hughe, the valet he then hired became one of Nazi Germany's most successful spies, codenamed 'Cicero'. And it was only after the war, when they had the chance to interview German intelligence officers in Berlin, that the British found out how close the Nazis had been to gaining details about the most secret operation of the war in Europe: the 1944 Allied invasion of Normandy.

The spy, Ilyas Bazna, served as Sir Hughe's valet from 20 July 1943 until early April 1944. Unfortunately for Sir Hughe, from October 1943 he was also supplying intelligence to the German ambassador Franz von Papen.

Reconstructing the details of the fiasco, the Foreign Office realized that the sole culprit was the ambassador himself. 'He was responsible for a serious leakage to the enemy because for a considerable time he kept highly secret papers in his box at home and carried the key on his person,' summarized an FO security expert, J.E.D. Street. It was a simple matter for Cicero to obtain an impression of the key which was cut for him in Berlin, and copy the box's contents as the opportunity arose. It certainly didn't help matters that Sir Hughe left the keys on his dressing table whilst taking his daily bath.

In a bid to nail the leaker, the FO went to the unique lengths of creating a false Cabinet paper, which they fed to Sir Hughe as genuine in the hope that Cicero would pick it up. The paper, entitled 'Peace Feelers from Bulgaria', was a neat piece of misinformation about a coup d'état being planned to remove the pro-German government in Bulgaria after the recent death of King Boris III. Watchers in London were disappointed as they waited for the German reaction to this news; none was ever detected.

After the war, two telegrams from Cicero were found in Berlin's archives that mention the code name for the Allied invasion, Operation Overlord. This is confirmed in papers relating to the interrogation of their translator, Fraulein Maria Molkenteller, held at the National Archives. By great good fortune, however, about the time Cicero's Overlord telegrams arrived in Berlin, the Gestapo was in the process of destroying the Abwehr, the German High Command's intelligence agency, and its head, Admiral Wilhelm Canaris, who had been implicated in several plots against Hitler's life.

The war over, the FO establishment pondered whether to court-martial Sir Hughe but ended up promoting him, appointing him ambassador in Brussels. A final paper in the archive describes Sir Hughe's efforts to ensure that his obituaries would not claim that he had blown the cover of Operation Overlord.

Cicero himself, who passed over almost 50 rolls of film of papers in Sir Hughe's secret boxes, did poorly from the whole arrangement. The Germans paid him off in counterfeit English notes made by their team of forgers in Sachsenhausen concentration camp. He appears to resurface in Istanbul in 1951, when a film then called *Operation Cicero* was being put together. (It was later released as *5 Fingers*, with Bazna's role taken by James Mason).

A Turkish newspaper report had it that Bazna was being expelled from the country, prompting a note in the FO file that asked quizzically: 'I wonder where he is being expelled to?' That story was later denied by the Turkish authorities and the final note in the file says simply: 'I think leave it.'

OUR DARKER DAYS

Foreign Office failed Cavell

The Foreign Office files that chronicle the case of Norfolk-born nurse Edith Cavell, condemned to death for treason by German forces occupying Belgium during the First World War, are stark and easy to follow. The story they reveal indicates that while the FO was informed of her arrest seven weeks before her execution in Brussels on 12 October 1915, it declined to put pressure on the Germans to show leniency.

Cavell was a well-known figure in the Belgian capital, where she ran a leading hospital that treated German and Allied soldiers without distinction. Convinced that captured British soldiers ran the risk of being executed, she aided some 200 to escape back to Britain by introducing them to a network of resistance fighters who escorted them to neutral territory in Holland. Her role came to the notice of the Germans when some of these men were arrested near the Dutch border. Challenged by the Germans, she freely admitted both her actions and her reasons for taking them.

When it became clear that the Germans were going to try her for treason, one internal Foreign Office memo commented blithely that 'the US minister will see that she has a fair trial', while another official wrung his hands ineffectually and stated that 'Miss Cavell will get a heavy sentence. There seems to be nothing to do.' Sir Horace Rowland, under-secretary to Secretary of State Sir Edward Grey, noted: 'I am afraid it is likely to go hard with Miss Cavell. I am afraid we are powerless.' Their do-nothing approach was backed by Lord Robert Cecil, formerly of the Red Cross but at this time Under-Secretary of State for Foreign Affairs. 'Any representation by us will do her more harm than good,' he advised.

The Americans, still neutral at this stage in the war, showed a great deal more energy and urgency. 'We neglected to present no phase of the matter which might have had any effect, emphasizing the horror of executing a woman no matter what her offence, pointing out that the death sentence had heretofore been imposed only for actual cases of espionage and that Miss Cavell was not even accused by the German authorities of anything so serious,' wrote an official, Hugh Gibson, to the US minister in Brussels, Brand Whitlock. One unintended consequence of Cavell's execution was to harden American opinion against the Kaiser at a time when the British were keen for the US to join the anti-German alliance.

Cavell's trial was held in camera, and the files contain several third-hand reports from people who witnessed it or the moments leading up to her execution. And while one might expect them to put on as brave a face as possible, the picture they paint of Edith Cavell is a highly moving one; she spoke clearly and openly about her actions and went before the firing squad, within hours of the military court's verdict being passed, fortified by a deeply held sense of pious expectation.

A modern reader might, however, be slightly troubled by the entire file. Were FO officials really afraid that if they contacted Berlin, either privately or publicly, Cavell would be worse off? Did they gamble on the gentle-manliness of the Germans and calculate poorly? Did local German military commanders behave harshly in a way their Berlin masters did not anticipate? This seems unlikely, as they were publicly backed by the German government after the event.

Despite being in close contact with the American Legation in Brussels it seems that the Foreign Office was not even able to inform Cavell's brother-in-law, Dr Longworth Wainwright, of the news of her death before he heard of it from another source. The files contain a letter from him saying that he'd received a wire on the 13th from a chaplain in Brussels announcing that 'Miss Edith Cavell died this morning'. 'Have you any information on what this implies?' the bewildered doctor asked.

A number of myths quickly grew up around Cavell's last moments. Stories describing how only one bullet of the firing squad's twelve had actually hit her and how a German officer had delivered the *coup de grâce* appeared in the *Manchester Guardian* less than a fortnight later.

The latter image was picked up in numerous pictorial representations circulating at the time.

Cavell's personal file, put together by the forerunner of MI6, contains poignant photos of her temporary grave at the Tir Nationale, the Brussels Execution Ground, and also a bizarre message passed on by a member of the Belgian aristocracy living in Berkshire to Cavell's mother in Norfolk, warning her not to mention to a red-haired cockney spy that her daughter was in Belgium.

A certain amount of hysteria hit the government also. The initial reaction was to label the execution as 'a sign of weakness' on the part of the Germans. One official commented that no female, even if accused of espionage, had received more than penal servitude from the British.

However, the mood also swung in reaction to a harsher stance. In the War Office one memo writer states as fact that there was already an increase in the number of female German spies, a claim later pooh-poohed by another. One official opined that it did not make sense to use the civil courts in Britain to try to convict a traitorous spy, far better to use a court martial as the Germans did. Nor did everyone in Britain wish to retain the high moral ground. 'I am advocating no vindictive methods,' wrote another five days after Nurse Cavell's execution, 'but in a clear case of female espionage we should not hesitate to apply the full penalty.'

Shot at dawn

One of the sorriest aspects of the First World War was the execution by firing squad of deserters and those deemed to be cowards or disobedient. A total of 306 British soldiers were executed under courts martial, plus 40 from the Commonwealth, out of some three thousand condemned to death.

As early as September 1914 the commander of the British Expeditionary Force (BEF), Sir John French, gave instructions to the courts martial that they were to consider not only the weight of the evidence before them but also the extra-judicial assessment of the state of discipline within the army. Thus the officers sitting in judgement were given the green light to set exemplary punishments *pour encourager les autres*. Furthermore, General Routine Order No. 585 sent to the BEF in January 1915 largely reversed the burden of proof by removing the presumption of innocence in cases of desertion and authorizing the court to assume guilt.

On top of these institutional obstacles to justice, many of those put on trial were not told of the possibility of clemency and were ignorant of their rights. Often the courts failed to investigate defence claims, and evidence of medical issues and other extenuating circumstances was ignored. The accused seemed to lack even a rudimentary understanding of their rights under military law, and in most cases no 'prisoner's friend' was found to safeguard them.

The death sentences were handed down by Field General Courts-Martial, a special system that took advantage of wartime conditions to dispense rapid justice. These were military trials convened in the field with a minimum of three officers, a captain or above acting as president. The sentence of death could not be passed without the unanimous agreement of all on the panel.

Since the release of the files on many of the deserters, a campaign has got under way to obtain a blanket pardon for all the men executed by their own forces during the First World War. Attention has focused especially on the disproportionately high number of Irishmen executed by the British military, a total of 26 soldiers, only one of whom apparently had legal representation.

A glance at these files is heart-rending. The proceedings are often recorded in faded pencil on scraps of paper that look as if torn from a child's notebook. The notes are so brief that it is hard to see how even the simple court-martial proceedings were followed to any extent.

One hearing involved Private Patrick Downey from Limerick and five other soldiers of the 6th Leinsters whilst they were billeted in Hasanli in Serbia. On 1 December 1915 Private Downey, in the words of the charge, was guilty of the offence of 'on active service disobeying a lawful command in such a manner as to show wilful defiance of authority given personally by his superior officer in the execution of his office'. It appears he refused to fall in and put his cap on when requested. Doubtless not realizing the potential consequences, Downey pleaded guilty in court. He was 19 and deemed by his officers to have a 'very bad' character.

As the decision to confirm his execution made its way up the chain of command, Lieutenant General Brian Mahon, the commander of British forces in Greece, wrote on 12 December that 'under ordinary circumstances I would have hesitated to recommend that the Capital Sentence awarded be put into effect as a plea of guilty has been erroneously accepted by the Court, but the condition of discipline in the Battalion is such as to render an exemplary punishment highly desirable and I therefore hope that the commander in chief will see fit to approve the sentence of death in this instance'.

Given the degree of horror, carnage and destruction that ordinary combatants faced in the war, official statistics show that in fact there was no major disaffection among front-line troops and that the High Command was worried about a problem that had not arisen. According to the campaign to win pardons for these men, during the four key years of the war there were fewer than 5,700 cases of desertion from the front and only 631 cases of mutiny out of an army of five million. In contrast, there were 31,000 desertions at home for which no soldier was shot.

Private Downey was executed at 08.00 hours on 27 December 1915 at Eurenjik, near Salonica, in Greece.

WO 71/441–2   WO 71/464–5

90

The conman who sold honours

In summer 2006 Scotland Yard detectives investigating a major government 'cash for peerages' scandal asked the National Archives for a file the police force had donated in 2003. It concerned Arthur Maundy Gregory, a prolific conman who brokered for David Lloyd George, Prime Minister from 1916 to 1922, the sale of honours to some of the most important men of the day. The scandal so rocked the nation that an Act to prevent the traffic was passed in 1925.

Maundy Gregory was undeterred by the legislation and continued soliciting cash for honours despite his inability to deliver them. He even diversified into the sale of obscure foreign orders and Catholic medals. Eventually, however, his extravagant lifestyle - including ownership of the hip Ambassador Club in Soho and Deepdene Hotel in Dorking - undid him, and in 1933 he was caught and put on trial. After receiving an exceptionally light sentence, he fled to Paris, where he died in a Nazi internment camp in 1941.

It is speculated that he got off so lightly because he had earlier worked as a spy for the infant MI5 and MI6 and knew such a wealth of secrets about establishment figures that it was in no one's interests to pursue him too vigorously.

THE HANGING BUSINESS

The glamour surrounding the post of hangman had been in decline long before Britain's last executions took place in 1964.

Back in the nineteenth century the chief hangman, William Calcraft, who served for nearly half a century from 1829 to 1874, was paid a guinea a week as a retainer for being the official hangman of London. On top of this handsome amount he received a guinea for each execution and half a crown for each flogging, and extra for travel to provincial cities.

By the 1930s the hangman's fee was negotiable, with the recommended level set at £10 plus a third-class railway fare. The inevitable result was that Britain's hangmen had to find supplementary income. When they sometimes failed to play by what the Home Office regarded as gentlemen's rules, they came in for severe criticism.

During the Great Depression period two rival hangmen were reprimanded for chasing business. When a newspaper recorded a capital sentence as having been passed in court, Thomas Pierrepoint and Robert Baxter wrote to the appropriate under-sheriff, the local official responsible for selecting the hangman for a specific execution. However, up to 90 per cent of capital sentences were commuted upon appeal, so in practice the hangmen were touting for business before it was certain that the sentences would actually be carried out. Although the under-sheriffs could select from any name on the official list of hangmen, which usually stood at around a dozen at any one time, there was clearly a pecking order that created difficulties for anyone trying to break into the business. A senior Prison Commission official wrote to the two men in 1927 ordering them to desist from 'the unacceptable behaviour of touting for business from under-sheriffs'. Tom Pierrepoint's reply the following year is preserved in the files: 'I never used to write but I found it out that some one else was and I was not getting my fair turn. The Junior man was getting the work and the Senior man was waiting idle.'

Thomas Pierrepoint dispatched more than 300 people during his 37 years in the post. He had taken over from his brother Henry, who was Chief Executioner before him, and in turn he trained Henry's son Albert, who became Britain's most prolific executioner of modern times. In his 24 years in office Albert executed at least 450 men and women, including some 200 Nazis at the end of the Second World War. In fact, the boost in income provided by his German work allowed him to sell his grocery shop and run a pub in Hollinwood near Oldham, which rejoiced in the ironic name of Help the Poor Struggler.

After Albert resigned, he lined up a highly lucrative series of articles in the *Empire News and Sunday Chronicle* in which he intended to reveal details of the last moments of some of the famous people he had dispatched, including Ruth Ellis in 1955, the last woman to be hanged, and John Amery in 1945, the last person to be executed for treason. However, when the Home Office got wind of this, they strongly disapproved and exerted pressure on the newspaper to drop the series.

Albert himself was opposed to capital punishment, not so much because it was wrong but because it was not an effective deterrent, and because the system of reprieve was politically driven rather than being based on the merits of each case.

Extraordinarily, in 1950 he executed a man called James Corbitt, who had been a regular at his own pub. Indeed, the two men had sung a duet of Danny Boy together before Corbitt left the pub and that same evening murdered his girlfriend in a fit of jealousy.

....

Social stain

In 1950 a woman in Plymouth had a child by a married man whom she subsequently married after he had divorced his wife.

Unable to get a birth certificate for her son with the father's name on it, she complained to the Home Office. Officials noted that when debating the 1926 Act of Legitimacy the Commons had been in favour of such an option, but the Lords resolutely opposed the idea.

One H.H. Savidge suggested that 'adoption is the most satisfactory expedient for protecting him now… It may even be better for him to believe that his parents "chose" him for adoption than to know that he is their own child born before their marriage.'

Half a century later approaching half of all children born in Britain have unmarried parents and this no longer carries a stigma.

Whisky galore!

The story of how a band of plucky Scottish islanders salvaged a cargo of shipwrecked whisky during the Second World War has almost become part of the British psyche, thanks to the 1949 black-and-white Ealing comedy *Whisky Galore!* Customs files, written by officials who were largely thwarted in their attempts to round up the contraband, reveal the fine detail of the islanders' Robin Hood activities.

The SS *Politician* was en route from Liverpool to Jamaica and New Orleans in February 1941 when, two days out of port, it ran aground in rough weather 150 yards off Calvay Island in the Sound of Eriskay in the remote Outer Hebrides. Locals recall that more than 20 members of the crew abandoned ship against the orders of the ship's master and were lucky to be rescued by the islanders of Eriskay. At this point accounts diverge.

Compton Mackenzie's book about the incident, upon which the film was based, portrays the islanders as overwhelmed by the strictures of wartime rationing. Unable to bear the waste on their doorstep of so much of the 'water of life', no fewer than 25,000 quart bottles of whisky, they did their best to rescue them from destruction. British customs officials, however, took a dim view of this salvage operation. Their search for looted liquor uncovered stashes in 'a peat hag', in crofters' outhouses, and buried in a garden. Some were even hidden in the sea; one official found eight sacks, each containing a case of quart bottles, weighted with large stones and lumps of coal and made fast by a cable to a rock onshore.

The ship was repeatedly visited over many months until it was finally moved. As early as 29 March one returning officer noted: 'I wouldn't have believed such a mess was possible. Every hatch was opened. Number 5

hold, where the liquor is, is open to the heavens.' At one point three boats carrying 42 cases of whisky were intercepted. On board one of the boats was an 84-year-old islander whom the writer thought should have his pension docked in recompense for his 'partially successful trip'.

Local accounts relate that the islanders held off approaching the wreck until after the sabbath and that the ship also carried a range of general goods, including bicycles and a large number of left shoes that were stored separately from the right ones to deter dockside pilferers. Later there were reports of navy ratings being spotted on board when they should have been guarding the wreck, and of aerodrome lorries trucking unearthed goods to the RAF station at nearby Benbecula. And no one owned up to finding any of the several hundred thousand ten-shilling notes that were meant to go into circulation in Jamaica, almost a quarter of which were never recovered or identified again.

The police correspondence lists indictments against 28 named islanders, one of whom was found with only a tin pail and three bundles of printed cotton, and contains discussions about how much offenders should have to pay to get their forfeited boats back. The chief constable of Inverness-shire constabulary made repeated complaints to the head of customs that 'uncustomed goods' were blocking his station in Lochboisdale and requested funds to cover the additional costs of 'special officers sent from the mainland'.

In November the decision was taken to detonate

explosives in hold number five to ensure, as an official put it, that 'no undutiable bottles remained'. The effect of the shipwreck continues, however, to reverberate to this day, and in the unlikeliest of places.

The 1949 film was the first major picture directed by Alexander Mackendrick, now recognized as Scotland's foremost film director. A Glaswegian Calvinist, when a discussion arose about the appropriate ending for the film, he sided with the thwarted customs officials, a view countered by the more liberal views of his Jewish producer. The film was shot in just three months on nearby Barra but owing to bad weather went hugely over budget to the point where it threatened the studio's existence. It turned out to be its most successful film of all time, even more so than the other two classics released that same year, *Passport to Pimlico* and *Kind Hearts and Coronets*. In the USA a cinema billboard ban on the word 'whisky' prompted a clever bit of word play in the change of name to *Tight Little Island*. But the biggest impact was felt in France, where the title used, *Whisky a Go Go*, launched a nightclub of the same name and is single-handedly credited with a shift in post-war French drinking habits.

The SS *Politician* is one ship that has had more influence as a wreck than it ever did when it was afloat, and 'whisky' and 'galore' are now the two best-known Gaelic words in everyday English. The film, meanwhile, has achieved the accolade that only the most successful earn: there are plans for a remake.

Schoolgirls spread wartime VD

When American troops arrived in Britain in 1942 to prepare for the liberation of Europe, they did not expect to meet danger so close to home – in the innocuous form of the British schoolgirl.

It was of course to be anticipated that the troops would attract female attention. Billeted in Mayfair at 100 Piccadilly, they were just around the corner from Shepherd's Market, a well-known haunt of prostitutes. And the GIs were facing a novel situation. In the USA prostitution was illegal and soliciting outlawed, but in more permissive Britain any solicitation had to cause offence before an arrest could be made. Moreover, clients were required to testify against the prostitutes they used, and opportunities for consensual contact were rife because London was in the grip of a strict nightly blackout.

Before long an American judge was demanding that the London police clear suspect women from the streets. He believed that 'the boys should be able to write home saying they never saw a doubtful lady in the streets of London'. The *New York Times* described Piccadilly as 'nightly transformed into a veritable open market', more akin to Genoa or Marseilles. It stated that in just four months some 2,000 soldiers had been rendered *hors de combat* through venereal disease, almost half of whom had been laid low by the 'Piccadilly commandos'.

Civilians were horrified by what they saw. One letter from an American reports that women and girls, some in their early teens, would 'pester American soldiers, clinging to their arms, refusing to be shaken off, telling stories of poverty, etc. An American officer told me he had never seen anything like it in France or anywhere else.' In response the US authorities froze part of the soldiers' pay to discourage indiscreet spending whilst 'in the holiday spirit'.

Senior British officials and the military found it hard to understand what the fuss was about. A 1942 Home Office memo suggested the cause of the problem was the 'quite remarkable inexperience of a large part of the American troops who succumb to the most elementary trick'. But for the press this culture clash was a story with legs. On 4 June 1943 the *Daily Mirror* ran an article about 'week-end girls' of 'good reputation' who frequented hotel lobbies until they found a new American friend, theorizing that the GIs were preferred for their money and naivety.

The police said that it was impossible to take action against the girls 'because they were not common prostitutes and did not accost; they simply made it clear they would welcome advances and this was not a criminal offence'. The files suggest that the police feared the fallout that would result if 'a respectable woman' was arrested by mistake.

It was into this melee that London's Metropolitan Police introduced another fear: the health risks posed by girls absconding from approved schools and heading to Soho to meet American GIs. A Superintendent Cole appears to have started this hare in April 1943, at a Home Office conference on solicitation by prostitutes, when he claimed that 'a good deal of trouble was caused in the West End of London by girls of 15–17 who had escaped from approved schools. Such girls, who were often suffering from venereal disease, after absconding, made their way to the West End of London and frequented undesirable cafes where they could strike up acquaintances with American soldiers who had plenty of money. These American soldiers passed the girls to their friends and in a very short time any one girl could be responsible for infecting a considerable number of people.' This complaint seems to have caused irritation at the Ministry of Health, which responded, in the person of a Dr Makepeace, by asking the Met for detailed figures to back up their assertions.

Other police officers attempted to strike a balance. Superintendent D. Peto, writing to a Miss Good in the Children's Branch of the Home Office, noted that 'although I agree with Superintendent Cole that the semi-delinquent type of girl and young woman, of which the Approved-School-failure forms a part, is a greater danger than the prostitute proper in regard to spreading venereal disease, I don't think that one should go to the other extreme and regard every Approved School absconder who is arrested in the West End as there for the purposes of immoral relations with Service men'. Clearly having second thoughts, she handwrote on the foot of her letter: 'Of course, some absconders are most definitely potential prostitutes.'

Investigating officials were by now beginning to get a little testy. 'Superintendent Cole does not seem to have given a true picture of the situation,' noted one, quoting figures of 13 senior and 8 junior absconders who 'came back requiring treatment' for VD in 1942. The number of abscondings totalled 900 (including, he points out, multiple events by some individuals), but only 116 cases of venereal disease were found that year in approved schools. The official concluded, somewhat witheringly, that 'absconders are rarely infectious when they abscond'. Having proved Superintendent Cole wrong, he noted that adding further security measures to prevent girls from absconding would cut right across the current policy of keeping the approved schools 'open'.

There is no record of what further action was taken, but the file bears all the hallmarks of one put on the shelf for good.

MEPO 3/2138 MH 102/895

102

THE FAMOUS
AND INFAMOUS

THE JAGGER

A creature which emerges from hiding once a year to
drive small females mad with its strange honking.
For the rest of the time it invests.

ROYAL SON COVER-UP

Few stories are more bizarre than that of the twenty-year campaign of Clarence Guy Gordon Haddon to be acknowledged as the natural son of Prince Albert Victor, the Duke of Clarence.

The Duke had a well-earned reputation in the 1880s as a bon viveur and womanizer. As the eldest son of the Prince of Wales, later Edward VII, he was in the direct line of royal succession, though his early death at the age of 28 meant that today 'Prince Eddy' is remembered, if at all, simply as the elder brother of King George V.

In 1889 Albert was rumoured to be implicated in the exposure of a high-class brothel in what became known as the Cleveland Street Scandal. Soon afterwards he was dispatched to India on a royal tour, where he may have begun a liaison with Haddon's mother, Margery. Some accounts have it that Mrs Haddon subsequently turned up in London claiming that she was carrying the Duke's child, that officials discreetly arranged her passage back to India and even that letters written to her by the Duke were purchased back by his lawyers.

Mrs Haddon later moved to Britain and was apparently arrested one day in 1914 outside the gates of Buckingham Palace shouting that she was the mother of the Duke of Clarence's illegitimate son. A memorandum in the four-inch bundle of Home Office (HO) files claims she then led 'a very disreputable life and went through forms of marriage with other people'. No one seems to know where and when she died, though as late as 1943 her son's nurse wrote to the Home Secretary, Herbert Morrison, claiming that she was being held captive in Edinburgh Castle.

Clarence Haddon seems to have worked in many places in Asia and South America, including a spell in the British army. He surfaces in 1929, when he published a book in America entitled *My Uncle, George V*, a copy of which lies in the HO file. This stimulated the rapid expansion of the files of the Metropolitan Police, as a blizzard of correspondence from Haddon to members of the royal family percolated back to Special Branch. One memo details the police's unsuccessful attempts to corroborate the assertions in Haddon's book. 'The author seems to have been unfortunate in regard to relevant records in support of his story,' the writer confides, noting that key letters from the Duke to Haddon's mother were allegedly 'among the contents of a bag stolen from him in 1912 on a voyage from Valparaiso to Taltal' and, more crucially, that 'there is no record of his own birth in London'. A search in Somerset House did, however, uncover the fact of Clarence Haddon's second marriage, in Sofia, Bulgaria, in 1923.

Behind the scenes, as the royal family doubtless made known their irritation at the demands for money and recognition that Haddon almost daily pressed upon them,

105

the matter was dealt with by the Keeper of the Privy Purse, the Metropolitan Police Commissioner and the head of Special Branch. In one letter to King George V in 1933 Haddon dared the Establishment to take him to court to challenge his version of events and signed himself 'I have the honour to be, Your Majesty, one of your own blood.' When he threatened to plaster his story on a billboard and parade through the West End of London, the police duly acted. In January 1934 Haddon was convicted of demanding money with menaces; he ended up getting twelve months with hard labour after he broke a condition that he desist from continuing with his claims.

The Medical Officer at London's Wormwood Scrubs prison describes Haddon as having 'a litigious, aggressive and irritable temperament, and he requires little or no invitation to discuss at great length the alleged injustice of his case'. He concluded that 'while there is evidence of mental disorder this is insufficient to enable him to be certified as insane', a comment later qualified by a handwritten note that simply added the words 'at present'.

In 1939 Haddon was still sending pamphlets to Queen Mary, who had once been engaged to the Duke of Clarence but had ended up marrying his brother George. Hadden died in 1943 under the impression that the Home Office was preventing his mother from visiting him.

Conspiracy theorists will be pleased to note that HO

records suggest that earlier papers relevant to the story had been destroyed. However, the police did prove to their own satisfaction that the dates of the Duke's visit to India and the boy's subsequent birth did not tally. What is not in doubt is the degree to which the story was embellished over time. In his 1929 book Haddon stated that his mother met the Duke in India, but by 1943 one of his supporters was claiming that Mrs Haddon had married the Duke in Ireland when he was a minor. And tucked away in the files is a letter, dated 1933, from the Deputy Police Commissioner in Bombay, one P. Wilkins, who had spotted a report of the Haddon trial in the *Times of India* and copied to his London colleagues an Indian government circular, dated 1906, refuting Mrs Haddon's royal claims.

One of the most poignant items in the HO file is a photo of Clarence Haddon, obtained by subterfuge by a policeman claiming to be a commercial traveller. In it Haddon looks like everyone's favourite uncle, not the deeply tormented man he clearly was. And perhaps the saddest thing of all is that even if he had been recognized, he could never have known his father. The Duke of Clarence died in 1892 during an influenza epidemic, when the little boy could have been but two or three years old.

HO 144/21778   MEPO 2/9552/1–2

Arthur Ransome: swallows and Soviets

Arthur Ransome, the author of the Lakeland classic *Swallows and Amazons*, seems an unlikely target for the attentions of the British security services. But the one-time *Daily News* and *Manchester Guardian* journalist had witnessed the October Revolution in St Petersburg in 1917 and married Leon Trotsky's private secretary, Evgenia Shelepin, as his second wife in 1924. A regular visitor to the Soviet Union after the revolution, he attracted suspicion as lavender attracts the bee.

Several security service files describe him as 'an ardent Bolshevik'. Others suggest that the author – code-named S76 – had in fact been asked to monitor leading Bolsheviks on behalf of the British government. Even so, it wasn't until 1937 that MI5 agreed that the by now famous man could be removed from its blacklist.

A roster of thrilling tales have attached themselves to Ransome. It was rumoured, for example, that he and Shelepin delivered a message from the Soviet leader, Lenin, to Estonian leaders in a bid to secure the Baltic seaboard for the Reds, and that the pair carried vast amounts of Red valuables with them when they left Russia.

Ransome was by all accounts a colourful character, good company and a bit indiscreet, a trait that surely disqualifies him from any serious accusation that he was a spy or double agent. A report from an informant on a boat to China in the 1920s says that 'it is not difficult to get him to talk – provided one is a good listener'. A British security official summed him up as 'one who reports what he sees, but as one who does not always see straight'.

Ransome originally went to Russia in 1912 to research folk fairy tales and escape a failed marriage. By 1917 he had earned a note from the British ambassador in Moscow saying that he had worked for the embassy for three years. The following year the attaché (and secret agent) Bruce Lockhart asked London for permission to put Shelepin on Ransome's passport as his wife so that they could leave secretly for Sweden. He described her as 'a very useful lady … she has been of the greatest service to me'.

The files are peppered with claims and counterclaims, requests for special favours for Ransome, official letters allowing him back into the country, reports from military men citing Ransome as an open Bolshevik and conciliatory memos from within the system claiming that he is only behaving so as a front. The resulting wonderful confusion was created by a man who made his living from telling tales. It seems unlikely that the truth about him will ever be crystal clear.

Criticizing
Amy Johnson

The first aerial circumnavigation of the globe, completed in 1924, took 175 days. In 1930 Amy Johnson, aged 27 and born in the year that Orville and Wilbur Wright first flew, set out to beat the then record of 16 days for the flight from London to Australia.

Johnson's De Havilland Gipsy Moth biplane, registration number G-AAAH, had a top speed of 102 mph. Her initial flight from Croydon aerodrome to Vienna was estimated at ten hours, and the trip to Australia planned in 25 hops over fourteen days. It would take 6 hops to reach Baghdad, 15 to arrive in the Burmese capital Rangoon and 18 to reach Singapore. Ahead of her then lay thousands of miles over the Dutch East Indies, now Indonesia, and large tracts of ocean uncrossed by commercial shipping routes. After a crash landing in Burma, her epic 11,000-mile journey took her 20 days; she missed the record but entered history as the first woman to make a single air journey from London to Australia.

Only informed of Johnson's plans in April, Britain's Air Council dispatched a memo to the Foreign Office requesting that it cable ahead for landing permission from the authorities in French Syria, Turkey and Persia. Keen to recoup costs, the FO ensured that charges for the cables were relayed back to the flier.

Johnson's success was by no means certain. The memo notes that 'no wireless apparatus or cameras will be carried in the aircraft' but that 'Miss Johnson will take with her a Browning pistol and 100 rounds of ammunition for use only in emergency'. No mention was made of the fact that she had been the first woman to gain a British ground engineer's licence, but officials did write to her as 'Miss Amy Johnson B. A.', her degree in economics from Sheffield University already marking her out as unusual.

Amy Johnson took off early in the morning of 5 May 1930. Files in the National Archives contain notes from officials along her route, many of whom commented on the 'great welcome' she received. But not all of them were entranced by her. 'It is impossible to view an undertaking of this nature, coupled with the sex, youth and comparative inexperience of the pilot, with other than mixed feelings', wrote our man in Sourabaya [sic] in Eastern Java, J. Drummond Hogg, somewhat testily. 'One is amazed that a girl alone should have got thus far safely in a machine of which the seating accommodation is scarcely roomier than a perambulator.' Hogg was firmly of the opinion that 'restrictions should, if possible, be placed upon such foolhardy enterprises' and, in conversation with Johnson, was incensed to find that she had no idea of local conditions, had only been flying for two years, and that before setting out from London her longest flight had been just four hours. She left Sourabaya, he fumed, 'the last place where repairs are possible', with an 'uncertain engine' and arrived many hours overdue at the next stop, Timor. 'I hope I may be forgiven for writing this dispatch which seems to decry the pioneering spirit for which we are justly famous, but I feel strongly (and others share my view) that adventuresses (I use the word in the good sense) like Miss Johnson should be protected against themselves and not permitted to venture alone upon such dangerous undertakings for purely selfish ends and with few other qualifications therefor [sic] than a dauntless courage.'

Another who shared Hogg's view was the acting consul-general in Batavia (modern-day Jakarta), H. Fitzmaurice. His summary to the FO noted that Johnson had missed the aerodrome at Sourabaya and landed 'in front of the sugar factory at Tjomal'. Lightening the load in her machine, she got airborne again the next day, met her luggage at an emergency runway she'd missed the night before and was then escorted en route to Sourabaya by a Dutch mail flight. She failed to arrive on time in Timor after coming down on a road. Having been given a severe telling-off in Sourabaya for not contacting the authorities to say that she would be late, this time she managed to phone ahead. 'It was just possible to cancel the search before planes left,' noted Fitzmaurice huffily before praising the Dutch, who kept their aerodromes open on a Sunday and worked until 4 am to help her mend her plane. Unlike him, they 'were almost disappointed that they were stopped from starting a search for a girl whose enterprise they admired so much'.

Such inconvenience was most vexing, and it took Fitzmaurice eight less-than-prophetic pages to vent his displeasure. 'The intrinsic utility of her enterprise is doubtful,' he concluded, 'its only value to the world generally would seem to lie in the advertisement it gives of the rapid progress civil aviation is making, which may well have its benefit to the revenues of air mail services.' The bureaucrat in Fitzmaurice would

doubtless have been pleased to note, however, that his recommendations were incorporated into subsequent Air Ministry instructions for aviation adventurers and aerial tourists.

Though she'd left England virtually unnoticed and failed to set a new solo record, Johnson was given a hero's welcome back in Britain as the first female aviator to fly the 10,000 mile journey single-handed to Australia. Her bottle-green Gipsy Moth, nicknamed Jason after her family's fish business, is today displayed in London's Science Museum. Johnson herself drowned in the Thames in January 1941 after she parachuted from the plane she was delivering to a nearby airfield as a member of the Air Transport Auxiliary. Ironically she was the first member of the ATA to die in wartime. Her body was never recovered.

Among the well-wishers who telegrammed congratulations to Amy Johnson in 1930 was a young aviator called Francis Chichester who went on to win a number of awards for long-distance flights in the Far East. In 1967 he completed the first circumnavigation of the world, with a single stop in Sydney, in his yacht Gypsy Moth IV, named in honour of Amy Johnson's plane. Chichester's voyage took nine months and one day; the current record for that 27,000 mile journey, set in 2005 by Ellen MacArthur, stands at just 71 days, a daily average only slightly less than Amy Johnson's pioneering flight.

THE SIMPSON DIVORCE

Edward, Prince of Wales, was a popular king-in-waiting. But when his father, George V, died in January 1936, it was clear that the government under Stanley Baldwin, the countries of the Commonwealth, the Anglican Church and the British people all had a much lower opinion of his proposed consort, the American divorcée Mrs Wallis Simpson.

Wallis and her husband Ernest Simpson had met the Prince in 1931. After acceding to the throne, King Edward VIII sought to maintain his position and reserve a place for Mrs Simpson, once she was divorced, but by the end of 1936 he had signed the instrument of abdication and left the country.

Central to these events is Wallis's divorce from Ernest Simpson. The typed transcript of the case in October 1936, held for convenience in Felixstowe, is just ten pages long. Mrs Simpson could only expect to be granted a divorce if her husband was caught in an adulterous liaison, a ground which Ernest had conveniently provided. Her suspicions, she told the court, were aroused when she read a compromising letter addressed to her husband. The proceedings took their formulaic turn, a staff member of the Hotel de Paris at Bray in Berkshire testifying that he'd served Mr Simpson and another woman breakfast in bed. Hard as it may be to believe today, the identity of the woman was not investigated.

An official called the King's Proctor had the duty to petition the court in divorce cases if he felt that their grounds had been fabricated. Many citizens wrote to him demanding that he investigate the ease with which Mrs Simpson's decree nisi was granted. Some repeated allegations that Mrs Simpson's first marriage was still valid, as she'd got divorced in Reno and a Nevada divorce was not recognized in the UK. Another revealed that on holiday in Austria the writer had met a hotel concierge who told him that Mrs Simpson and the Prince of Wales, travelling incognito in 1935, had 'occupied communicating rooms'.

In the end, the King's Proctor made no intervention, though he reported that he would have liked to interview Mrs Simpson's maid but that this was impossible as 'servants still in the employ of any person owe a duty to their employer, and it is not the position of the King's Proctor, and indeed it would be improper for him, to endeavour to get information from such servants'.

The Duke and Duchess of Windsor spent the rest of their lives in France; he died in 1972 and she followed him in 1986. Kept at a distance in life from the royal house they so nearly destroyed, in death they lie together behind the Royal Mausoleum in Windsor Home Park.

Big Brother watched Orwell

Documents in the National Archives reveal that the Special Branch of the Metropolitan Police kept George Orwell, the author of the anti-totalitarian masterpiece *Nineteen Eighty-Four*, under surveillance for a period of more than twelve years.

The MI5 file opens with a letter reporting the suspicions of the Chief Constable of the county borough of Wigan in 1936, when the writer, under his real name of Eric Arthur Blair, was carrying out research into the condition of the working class for a book that became *The Road to Wigan Pier*.

A Special Branch report in January 1942, when Orwell was working for the Indian Section of the BBC, describes him as having 'communist views', a political outlook evidenced by the observation that 'he dresses in a bohemian fashion both at the office and in his leisure hours'.

Olivier's tax coup

In September 1943 the actor Laurence Olivier was in an extremely powerful position. His contract to produce, direct and star in the film *King Henry V* gave him control over its publicity and almost every aspect of its creation. Not only would he earn a £100,000 fee, but he'd also get a 20 per cent share in the profits.

The film company backing the project, Two Cities Ltd, was sure that the film would be a great success, capturing as it clearly did the patriotic mood of the time. It may seem strange today, however, now that the film is an acknowledged classic, that when it was first shown in England in December 1944, it was slow at the box office. So in July 1945, facing a loss on the project, the film company took the unusual step of signing a separate agreement with Olivier that stopped him from making another film for eighteen months. This was designed to prevent any new Olivier film from further harming the ticket sales for *Henry V*.

Under the restriction agreement Olivier was paid £15,000, a sum close to half a million pounds in today's money, and he undertook to remain a British citizen and stay in the UK rather than move back to America. The nature of the contract became public after his accountants claimed that the sum was not remuneration for professional services and therefore should not be taxed. The Inland Revenue thought otherwise, arguing that a payment not to perform was a 'professional receipt' in the same way as a fee to perform was. This was no small matter in the days of high personal taxation rates.

The case went all the way to the Court of Appeal in 1951, with each court finding for Sir Laurence, as Olivier by then was. Summing up, the Appeal judge found that the money paid did not represent 'profits or gains from his vocation as an actor but rather a payment for abstaining from that vocation'. The Revenue, perhaps understandably, felt this flew in the face of common sense. 'I find it difficult to say what this reward is if it was not a receipt of the vocation,' noted one official, who felt that Sir Laurence 'exercises his vocation by refraining from acting as well as acting'.

Technically, *Henry V* was both quirky and clever. It was driven along by William Walton's energetic score, while the careful editing of the script had removed all the ambiguities in the young king's character as created by Shakespeare and turned the frivolity of the French court into an overweening confidence that chimed more closely with the behaviour of the current enemy, Nazi Germany. Wartime shortages meant, for example, that the knights' chain mail at the battle of Agincourt had to be made out of grey knitted wool. But the overall result, in early Technicolor, struck contemporaries, such as *Time* magazine's film reviewer James Agee, as masterful. Agee wrote prior to its US opening that 'United Artists, uneasy about the mass audience, is handling the film timidly'. Nonetheless, the film's popularity began its inexorable rise after a run in New York in June 1946.

Olivier went on to have a glittering film and stage career, though according to some accounts he was disappointed with his achievements. His three famous Shakespeare films, *Henry V*, *Hamlet* and *Richard III*, have introduced Shakespeare to more than one generation of post-war British schoolchildren. Among the great movie roles he was considered for were those that made James Mason famous in *Lolita* and Marlon Brando in *The Godfather*. After his death in 1989 Lord Olivier was buried in Westminster Abbey.

Diana Dors and the Home Secretary

The 1948 film *Good Time Girl* is today best known for helping to launch the screen career of Diana Dors in a bit part. It tells the story of a misfit schoolgirl who falls in with a bad crowd, ends up in a reformatory and inevitably descends into perdition.

When the film was first shown it caused consternation within the Home Office because of its harsh and inaccurate portrayal of life in reform schools. The Labour Secretary of State for Home Affairs, John Chuter Ede, was a former teacher and made it a personal quest to have the film changed before it was released. The film-maker's position was not helped by some lurid publicity that linked the subject matter to a notorious contemporary case of a young girl taken in by American GIs.

A review of the files shows that while officials were sensitive to the potential abuse of their powers, they were determined to rectify the matter. Alerted to the film's content by several letters of protest triggered by a preview article in the *Picture Post*, Ede wrote to the studio head, Arthur Rank, pointing out that the dramatic licences taken in the film distorted reality too far. Citing several factual errors – 'the girls wearing some uniform dress which might have been seen many years ago in a

121

reformatory' – Ede was especially irritated because the producers had asked his department for access to a number of institutions in order to ensure that their portrayal was accurate. Appealing to Rank 'as a Justice', Ede chides him that 'it is not so clear that parents of children, especially girls, will feel confidence in the schools if the impression is given that the story of this film is the normal history of dealing with those who come before our Juvenile Courts'.

The Chairman of the Board of Film Censors, Sir Sidney Harris, commented that ordinarily they would not 'reject the film on the grounds that it misrepresents the Approved School system', though personally he felt it was 'a sordid and undesirable story of the kind which is common in American films'. Warning Ede that, if faced by questions in Parliament, he would have to say that the film 'traduced the British system of dealing with young offenders', Harris observed that 'censorship cannot be used for the purpose of preventing misrepresentations of this kind. Freedom in the matter of propaganda necessarily involves freedom to misrepresent.'

Viewing reports, script amendments and correspondence flew to and fro for some months, before Ede, exasperated, drafted a note to Rank pointing out that 'if I knew of a school resembling that depicted in the film, it would be my duty at once to close it'.

Officials and Ede thought that Rank was trying to help them, but a modern reader is struck by how ineffectual his interventions were. One letter to Ede in which he writes 'I agree with you this is not satisfactory and I have talked to the Producer and am having it altered' sounds promising, before it concludes, tongue in check, 'so that it will be of help to your great purpose of making the teaching profession in Approved Schools a vocation'.

In the end, the film was panned by the critics. Milton Shulman of the *Evening Standard* summed it up as a 'bad girl makes worse film'. And he didn't even mention Diana Dors.

••

Jack Straw's visit to Chile

Former Labour Foreign Secretary Jack Straw is immortalized in papers chronicling a student union visit to Chile in 1966 to build a youth centre.

According to A.J.D. Stirling of the British Council in Santiago, it 'was a thoroughly disorganised affair. The party of students was nearly sent home in disgrace. The students were, as individuals, pleasant and intelligent; but considering that their average age was 23, that they were student leaders and that they had, I gather, been through some form of selection for this project, they were depressingly immature … their childish politicking and the disorganisation to which they arrived hastened the splitting of the party into quarrelling factions.'

'We had the impression that Jack Straw, the appropriately named chief trouble-maker, was acting with malice aforethought … he seemed deliberately to have brought matters to the point where the British council had to intervene.'

123

JAGGER: BUTTERFLY ON A WHEEL

Among recently released files relating to old headline-grabbing scandals are several with details from the Director of Public Prosecutions (DPP) and the Metropolitan Police about the arrest and trial of Mick Jagger and Marianne Faithfull on drugs charges following a raid on their Chelsea home in Cheyne Walk in May 1969.

They were busted by the head of the Chelsea Drugs Squad, Detective Sergeant Robin Constable. Jagger alleged that he had been framed and that Constable later offered him a deal for £1000 to drop the charges with the words: 'Don't worry about it Mick, we can sort it all out.' Scotland Yard launched an inquiry into the encounter after the Australian police reported in August 1969 that Faithfull had told them that she 'hated coppers' because she and Mick had been framed by the London police. The framing and deal allegations were mentioned again when the drugs bust case came to court in January 1970. There it was one man's word against another's and Jagger was fined £200 for possession of cannabis plus costs of fifty guineas.

The papers on the DPP's inquiry into the framing allegations in February 1970 reveal that Jagger's claims had caused some concern, not least because the rock star's counsel was the future Conservative Attorney-General Michael Havers. Jagger was also supported by a statement from left-wing MP Tom Driberg. In the end, however, the DPP decided to take no further action.

The establishment was somewhat wary of Jagger by this time, as the Drugs Squad had launched an earlier raid in 1967 after being tipped off by the *News of the World*. That court case saw Jagger and fellow guitarist Keith Richards given three months with hard labour. An editorial in *The Times* by William Rees-Mogg subsequently argued that they had been targeted because of their celebrity and, quoting Pope, asked 'Who breaks a butterfly on a wheel?' On appeal the convictions were overturned.

In the summer of 1969 the Rolling Stones was just about to release the single 'You Can't Always Get What You Want'. Police files of the day were ready to describe the band's friends as 'the dregs of society'. Though already famous, the band members were a long way from being the established figures that they are today, with a knighthood for Sir Mick and annual sales worth tens of millions of pounds.

Knobbling Bobby Moore

It was the kind of trick one might expect in South America. Bobby Moore, captain of the England football team, was arrested in Colombia on the eve of the 1970 World Cup in Mexico, accused of stealing a £600 bracelet 'encrusted with diamonds and emeralds' from a store in the team hotel in Bogota. And he'd only been in the country for two and half hours.

Immediately after his arrest it seemed that the mistake had been cleared up. But Moore was unexpectedly arrested as the plane carrying the England team touched back down in Bogota for a stopover on the way from Quito to Mexico for the opening game.

A shocked nation refused to believe the accusation. Files reveal that within weeks of Moore's arrest officials from the British embassy were told by local police that their suspect was, in fact, a woman with links to the criminal underworld. Quite how Moore's shopkeeper accuser managed to mistake the England captain for this woman is never explained directly, though the embassy report that went back to the Foreign Office commented darkly that 'the antecedents of the jeweller and his witnesses had been thoroughly scrutinized and some suspicious circumstances established'.

British interest in the case went right to the top. 'Every minute's delay in securing Moore's release militates against England's world cup chances,' wrote the head of the Football Association, Denis Follows, to the Prime Minister, Harold Wilson. The PM, who hoped that a second England win would give him a pre-election ratings boost, records his irritation at the 'growing evidence of delay caused by administrative inefficiency'.

British diplomats worked hard to get the allegation against Moore dropped, whilst noting that under the Colombian justice system 'only 20% of penal cases are finally settled'. As the Cup's opening match approached, they even visited Colombia's security chief to persuade him to warn the judge presiding over the case of the consequences if Moore were to be detained for much longer. He was eventually released in time to play in the tournament, but the files were still open in court as late as January 1971 and only in 1975 did the FO inform Moore that the case had been finally closed.

The files are full of details about how British diplomats tried to assist Moore despite some voices in London arguing for distance. 'Public opinion will never consider that this is just a legal case' was, however, the line from Bogota. There were specific worries that the use of the diplomatic bag to carry letters between Moore and his Colombian lawyer might contravene the Vienna Convention, though it was also observed that 'bag rules do get stretched in the national interest'. Bogota was advised to try to 'wean the lawyer away from this'.

Despite Moore's presence England exited the 1970 World Cup in the last eight after going down to their nemesis, West Germany, in extra time.

FCO 7/1634–5   FCO 53/120   PREM 13/3497

FINDING OUT MORE

The best source of information on the National Archives is its website: www.nationalarchives.gov.uk. There you will find details of new document releases as well as the catalogue, online documents, and guidance for researchers at all levels.

The Freedom of Information (FOI) Act 2000 has opened up a wealth of information to all. It applies to information whatever its age, whether it is held by the National Archives or the government department that created it. The 30-year closure period no longer determines access; instead, information is assumed to be 'open' from the start unless one of the Act's exemptions applies.

Public bodies are required to transfer selected files to the National Archives before they are 30 years old. As a result of the FOI Act most of the files are open on transfer. This means that every day new files are made available to the public at the National Archives either through standard transfer or following an FOI request. Additionally, there are two annual releases of MI5 documents – which do not come under the FOI Act – plus a large transfer of files at the end of each year.

Members of the press are regularly invited to view the more interesting files released – so watch out for revelations in tomorrow's news. Or why not take a look at the documents yourself – you might find your very own 'state secret'!